HELPING COUPLES CREATE GREAT MARRIAGES

BETTER TOGETHER

Design by: Jessica Amsberry

ISBN 9781635820683
ISBN 9781635820836

FIRST EDITION

Note: Individuals and couples cited as examples in this work are all real, gathered from a variety of sources. However, unless otherwise noted, all of their names and circumstances have been modified to protect their identities.

This project began with a dream: to create the best marriage preparation and enrichment experience in the world. For the millions of couples who will experience this program we hope we have delivered on that dream.

Hundreds of people have poured their time, talent, and expertise into BETTER TOGETHER. It is the result of years of research, development, and testing. To everyone who has contributed in every stage of the process: Thank you! May God bless you and reward you richly for your generosity.

Special thanks to: Jack Beers, Claire Darnell, Katie Ferrara, Anita Hunt, Lamar Hunt, Jr., Jennifer Miller, Mark Moore, Lindsey Schrock, Fr. Bob Sherry, and Ben Skudlarek.

Beyond the enormous talent contributions, others have been incredibly generous with their money. BETTER TOGETHER was funded by a group of incredibly generous donors. It will now be made available at no cost to every parish in north America. This is one of the many ways that this program is unique.

Everything great in history has been accomplished by people who believed that the future could be better than the past. Thank you for believing!

Now we offer BETTER TOGETHER to the Church as a gift, hopeful that it will help couples build great marriages.

BETTER TOGETHER is brought to you by Dynamic Catholic with special thanks to Dominick Albano, Lisa Brenninkmeyer, Allen Hunt, Corynne Staresinic, Sarah Swafford, and Matthew Kelly.

Designed by: The Dynamic Catholic Design Team
Principal Designer: Jessica Amsberry

Table of Contents

WELCOME

Something wonderful is about to happen to you. God dreams for your marriage to be the greatest source of peace, comfort, and joy in your life. Your marriage will have a powerful impact on your friends and family, the neighborhood you live in, the company you work for, the parish you are a part of, your future children, the schools they attend, and the whole world.

BETTER TOGETHER is designed to help you have the best marriage possible. You are holding in your hands the result of thousands of hours of rigorous research, development, and testing. More than 500 people have been involved in the process. Couples, facilitators, psychologists, mentor couples, and pastors have told us what is working and what isn't throughout the development of this program. Over and over, we have refined our offering based on their feedback.

Each of the 12 sessions you are about to experience is designed with 60 minutes of content for you. Here is what to expect:

WISDOM FROM. . .

At the start of each session you will find a story that shares the wisdom of real-life experience pertaining to the topic. Read through these on your own either before or after each meeting.

PRAYER

Begin each session with the prayer found on the inside of the front cover.

VIDEO

Each session starts with a short video sharing wisdom from our presenters

WATCH AND DISCUSS

Within each of the 12 sessions, you will find 5 segments, each including a brief video and ending with an exercise for you. Some of these exercises are designed to be done together as a couple, some done on your own individually.

Keep in mind that this content can be adapted to fit your needs. You can adjust the amount of material you cover to fit your schedule.

One of the most incredible gifts God has given us as human beings is the ability to dream. Unlike any other creature, we can look into the future, imagine something bigger and better, and then come back into the present and work to make that richly imagined future a reality.

At Dynamic Catholic our dream is that the Catholic family would be a beacon of hope for society. And we believe that at the heart of your family is your strong marriage.

As you begin this journey toward preparing for a beautiful and strong marriage, it is our privilege to make this journey with you. Thank you.

May the grace of our generous God inspire you and give you courage, wisdom, and patience.

The Dynamic Catholic Team

PRESENTERS

Multiple people have contributed their own stories and experiences to enrich this program. Here are the five you will find throughout this workbook:

———————————

DOMINICK ALBANO

Dominick Albano is a writer and speaker at Dynamic Catholic. Dominick and his wife, Rebecca, have been married for 11 years.

LISA BRENNINKMEYER

Lisa Brenninkmeyer is the founder of Walking with Purpose. Lisa and her husband, Leo, have been married for 26 years.

SARAH SWAFFORD

Sarah Swafford is a speaker and author of the book, *Emotional Virtue: A Guide to Drama-Free Relationships.* Sarah and her husband, Andrew, have been married for 13 years.

ALLEN HUNT

Allen Hunt is the Senior Advisor at Dynamic Catholic and author of the book, *The 21 Undeniable Secrets of Marriage.* Allen and his wife, Anita, have been married 30 years.

CORYNNE STARESINIC

Corynne Staresinic is the founder of The Catholic Woman. Corynne and her husband, Nick, have been married for 2 years.

*To see more of these contributors, go to **DynamicCatholic.com/ViewProgram***

Love does not consist of gazing at each other, but
in looking outward together in the same direction.

—Antoine de Saint Exupery

God's Dream for Marriage

SESSION 1

Wisdom for the Vows from Carlton and Maggie

You need wisdom to have a great marriage. And that wisdom doesn't just find you; you have to seek it out. I search for marriage wisdom nearly everywhere I go, with the people I meet and in the marriages I see.

When I first encountered the story of Carlton and Maggie, my wife and I had been married only a few years. As I heard it, I wrote it down. I wanted to hang on to the wisdom of this couple and draw from it for the rest of my life and for the rest of my family's life.

Carlton and Maggie met a long time ago in the rolling foothills of southern Ohio, near the Ohio River. Carlton was nine years old when his father gathered his kids to go to a funeral. A neighbor had died, leaving behind a widow and four small children.

After the funeral, as children moved around the burial site, Carlton noticed little seven-year-old Maggie standing with her grieving family. "That's sad," he thought, "such a poor thing, now with no daddy." And Carlton right then vowed to himself to keep an eye on her in the days and years ahead.

Soon, Carlton and Maggie saw each other every day. They were both part of a group of kids who walked to school together, traveling a mile down the road to their school each day.

Their friendship grew as each year passed. Carlton finished eighth grade and quit school so he could help his family tend the crops on their farm. Maggie eventually became a teacher in the rural schools of Ohio. They began courting. And together they went to church.

When Carlton turned twenty-four, he left the farm and moved to Pittsburgh to work in the mills. He needed to earn money, more than his family's small farm could provide. So he began as a shoveler. He did well enough that four years later, he and Maggie were married.

The couple and their families and friends gathered in the local church. An old retired priest, Father Newman, celebrated the Mass. He had to sit through most of the wedding because he was past the age of eighty by then.

Before the Mass, Father Newman leaned over to Carlton and said, "When I pray over you as man and wife, hold Maggie's hand and don't ever turn her loose." Carlton did just as he was told.

To have and to hold from this day forward.

Afterward, they all celebrated with cake and lemonade, and the newlyweds spent the night in her mother's home. They visited the next day with Carlton's family, and enjoyed fried chicken and more cake. The day after that, the couple headed back to Pittsburgh, so Carlton could return to work and Maggie could begin settling into her new home.

Carlton went back to work at the mill, in a city filled with smoke belching from the factories. Maggie was lonely in her new environment, and she often reminisced about all the old folks back home.

For better, for worse.

But things got better. She and Carlton found their new parish, with couples their age, and friendships that provided fellowship, some of which lasted the rest of their lives.

Times were tight. Carlton worked hard. Maggie handled the finances, and struggled to save a nickel here and a dime there.

For richer, for poorer.

It was not long before they were expecting their first child. And Maggie was fine until one morning in mid-May.

After breakfast that morning, Maggie doubled over in pain. Carlton rushed her to the hospital. An hour passed, then another. He anxiously kept vigil in the waiting room while the doctor tried, desperately and successfully, to save both Maggie and the baby inside her.

The baby was born breech, and the process did much damage to Maggie's small body, but the nurse brought Carlton a baby boy to meet out in the waiting room. He and Maggie named the boy Thomas and called him Tommy.

The years passed quickly, with Carlton spending long hours at the steel mill and working his way up the ladder from shoveler to supervisor. Tommy grew up. He went to college, joined the army, was stationed in California, and got married.

Eventually, Carlton retired, and he and Maggie soon moved to Fresno, California, to be near Tommy and his family. The pace of life slowed for Carlton and Maggie. They registered in the parish there and watched their two granddaughters grow up.

The calendar moved forward. Carlton cared for Maggie through breast cancer, cataract surgery, and two broken hips. Eventually, he did all the cooking. He washed, dried, and folded the clothes. He bathed her, because her vertebrae had collapsed from osteoporosis.

In sickness and in health.

One August evening, Carlton turned off the television and they headed for bed, but then Maggie collapsed in pain. Carlton frantically called 911 and waited. At the hospital, Maggie had emergency surgery for a perforated ulcer.

Afterward, she simply needed more care than Carlton could provide her. The family made the decision to move her to Hope Community Home, a care facility not too far from their home. Maggie soon made friends with all the nurses and residents. She was an easy patient—sweet, loved to laugh, and never complained.

Maggie's room was large enough so that Carlton was able to bring his rocker from home and place it beside her bed. It was the same rocker they had brought from Pittsburgh. The gentle creak of that chair comforted Maggie as she lay in the bed and Carlton sat nearby.

Maggie grew weaker and weaker. Carlton continued to feed her three times a day. He agonized over whether to move in with her but instead moved in with Tommy and his wife. Three times a day Carlton drove to be with Maggie at the care home. He still fed her each meal. When he gave up his driver's license on his ninety-second birthday, he relied on the city van to drive him to the home so he could feed Maggie each meal and sit in that rocker beside her.

Carlton rinsed her dentures, he stuffed pillows around her body in the wheelchair, and he gently dried her hair. Each Christmas, he purchased her two new house-dresses. He placed flowers in her honor at their church.

Maggie began to get more and more confused. She was not sure who or where she was. The more she failed, the more frantic Carlton became. Finally, the doctor told him, after five years of feeding her every meal, that Carlton was going to have to slow down. So he cut back to two visits per day.

On January 23, the family met with the doctor. The news was not good. Maggie had pneumonia, and she had stopped eating. The doctor told them that she was nearing the end.

From that moment on, Carlton was at her side constantly, at first saying, "Maggie, don't die. Please don't leave me."

Then, he began to accept that what she needed most was reassurance, so he said, "It's all right, honey. I'm right here. This is Carlton. I love you."

January 27 was a Sunday. Tommy went to church and received the Eucharist. Everyone in church knew why Carlton wasn't there. After the Mass, Tommy and their pastor joined Carlton to bring him Communion and to anoint Maggie. Peace settled over them all.

They left. Carlton remained behind, holding Maggie's hand.

He leaned against the bed. "Goodbye, Maggie," he said softly.

With her small hand resting in his, just as it had on the day they were married, Maggie breathed her last breath.

Until death do us part.

A few days later she was laid to rest with a small box at her side. Inside the box was the faded pink dress she had worn sixty-six years earlier on the day they were married, when she had said she loved Carlton enough to share the rest of her life with him.

God's Dream for Marriage

Why Are You Here?

Why are you here?

I don't ask this in some huge philosophical way, like "Why are you alive?" I mean: Why are you here, right now, going through marriage preparation?

Before you answer, let's set an expectation from the very beginning. You be honest with me, and I'll be honest with you. I'll start:

Honestly, I only remember five words from my marriage preparation experience:

"When you fight, fight naked."

These are the only words that struck me as I sat at the small table in the parish office with my pastor and bride-to-be. Needless to say, I didn't get a whole lot out of my marriage preparation experience. It might not need to be said, but those five words were not the best advice for a number of reasons.

But in the spirit of being honest, while I didn't have the best marriage preparation experience, I also didn't expect much out of it. Maybe I just didn't think the Church could really help me prepare for marriage. But the truth is I didn't expect much.

Honestly, many couples don't expect to get much out of their marriage preparation experience. It's good to acknowledge that many of us are here only because we have to be. I know that was true for me. Even those of us who care deeply about our faith tend to look at marriage preparation as a hoop to jump through—just one more box we have to check off so they will let us get married.

But ultimately we all want a great marriage. I don't think many engaged couples hope their marriage will be unhealthy. The divorce rate in America is often cited as 50 percent, but I think it's safe to say the percentage of engaged couples who hope they will get divorced is closer to 0.

You want a healthy marriage, I want you to have a healthy marriage, and the Church wants you to have a healthy marriage. Better still, God wants you to have a great marriage.

So honesty is a good place to start, because it is at the heart of a healthy marriage. If you don't have honesty up front, you don't have much.

So, right from the start, let's answer two fundamental questions.

First, why are you here?

Take some time to really consider the question. If you are here only because you have to be, that's OK. Don't be shy about that. Sometimes the best prayer we can pray is something like: God, I don't feel like praying right now.

The second question I want to invite you to consider: Why are you getting married?

Both these questions point toward something important: our purpose. We all have a purpose for marriage preparation. The Church has a purpose in inviting you to marriage preparation, and it's more than just giving you another hoop to jump through. I have a purpose in going on this journey with you. And truly, God has a purpose for your marriage preparation experience.

Thanks for letting me be on this journey with you. The days ahead are going to be some of the best of your life and it's my privilege to be a part of it.

Discuss:

Begin by getting really honest about these two questions.

1. Why are you here in marriage preparation?

2. Why are you getting married?

Talk to your bride-to-be about them. Share your answers with your future husband. Tell your beloved why you want to be married to her. Share why you are excited to be marrying your husband-to-be.

If a man and a woman marry in order to be companions on the journey through earth to heaven, then their union will bring great joy.

—St. John Chrysostom

God's Dream for Marriage

Better Together

I may not really know you, and you may not really know me, but there is one thing we both know for sure: We want to be the-best-version-of-ourselves.

Think about it. No one ever says they want to be a-second-rate-version-of-themselves. No one says they want to be the-worst-possible-version-of-themselves. Of course not. Given the choice, we all want to be the-best-version-of-ourselves. This truth is universal. So it should come as no surprise that our deepest desires align with this central truth. We all want to be the-best-version-of-ourselves.

Think about this:

You sit down for lunch at your favorite restaurant and you begin to check out the menu. Your eyes settle on a picture of a perfectly cooked half-pound burger covered in cheese, bacon, and a fried egg, served on a pretzel bun with a mountain of fries on the side. Your mouth begins to water just looking at it. But when the waitress comes, you order the Cobb salad and a glass of water with lemon. Why? Because your desire to be healthy and to live to walk your daughter down the aisle of her own wedding is deeper than your desire for that burger. Your desire to be healthy is oriented toward becoming the-best-version-of-yourself.

Or maybe you get home from a long day of work and don't even bother to flip on the lights before flopping onto the couch. You grab the remote, find the latest series everyone is talking about, and think about how many hours of sleep you can lose without making tomorrow too miserable. But before you hit play, you turn off the TV. You grab your phone and call your mom, and after talking to her for a bit you go to bed at a sensible time. What happened there? Sure it's an attractive idea to just crash on the couch and veg out, but your deeper desire is for stronger relationships with the people who matter most, and for rejuvenating sleep.

You get the point. The things that are ultimately most attractive to us are those things that help us become the-best-version-of-our-selves. So, let me ask you an honest question:

What do you find attractive about your beloved?

....

....

....

....

....

....

....

....

....

....

I'm sure your list could get pretty long pretty quickly. You might have a mix of everything from your physical attraction to each other to your personalities to the beauty of the other's heart. They are good and beautiful parts of every relationship. But you would also recognize that some of these things we are attracted to run deeper than others. For example, I am attracted to my wife's long, silky brunette hair, but she could go bald from cancer treatment and it wouldn't change how much I love her.

On a very deep level, we are attracted to our spouse-to-be because they make us a-better-version-of-ourselves. Why do you think so many love stories have some version of this scene: Prince Charming finally chases down the love of his life—in the rain, of course—and declares his love for her to the world. He stares deeply into her eyes and cries out, "You make me a better man!" Of course, she runs to him and they kiss and live happily ever after.

And really, you shouldn't be surprised that you make each other better. Why? Because God made you for each other.

God made you and you are good. God made you in his image. Male and female he created you. And he made you to be joined together as one. You were made to be good for each other.

That's why God has brought you together. He has a dream for the two of you. He dreams that you will become all that he created you to be and that you will live a good and full life. God wants you to help your future husband or wife become the-best-version-of-themselves too. That's the whole purpose of marriage: to help the two of you become the-best-version-of-yourselves.

This is God's dream for your marriage. He dreams that you will help each other become holy. God dreams that you will be better together.

Discuss:

Think about how you make each other better. Take a few minutes to finish the following statements and discuss some of your thoughts:

She makes me a better person by. . .
He makes me a better person by. . .

You have a deep desire to become the-best-version-of-yourself, and your future spouse is going to help you become the-best-version-of-yourself. Nothing is more attractive than that.

God's Dream for Marriage

1.1
1.2
1.3
1.4
1.5

How Do You Like Being Lied To?

How do you like being lied to?

Most people don't care much for being lied to. And how do you view the person who lied to you?

If someone lied to you once, you might be willing to forgive that. You might give the person the benefit of the doubt. Maybe they made a mistake. Maybe they regret it. Maybe they thought they were helping you by lying to you. But if that person lies to you another time, and another, then pretty soon you are going to grow fairly suspicious of them. You will be much slower to trust what they say.

How would it feel if someone lied to you all the time? If you had a major event going on in your life, would you turn to that person for advice? If they offered you advice, how seriously would you take it? After all, they have lied to you time and again.

Our culture is that person. Your whole life the culture has been telling you that your life is all about you. It has been lying to you with the individualism that only asks, "What's in it for me?" It has been misleading you with hedonism and its motto, "If it feels good, do it!" The culture has sought to deceive you with minimalism, the idea that somehow you can exert minimum effort and get maximum results. And it has lied to you with its relativism and the idea that what is true for you does not have to be true for me or for anyone else.

Individualism, hedonism, minimalism, and relativism. These are just four of the ways that the culture has been lying to you over and over again. And these four huge lies are all enemies of a great marriage. And they are enemies of a great life. Because all four of these ways of thinking leave you empty and dissatisfied.

Life is not me-centric, and marriage is certainly not me-centric. The culture tells you that marriage is about you and meeting your needs. You are filled with hopes and dreams about your future together, but the culture wants to turn those hopes and dreams into hopes and dreams about only yourself.

What will you get out of marriage? How will it benefit you? How will your husband or wife make you feel better, or take care of your wants and desires, or advance your personal interests? These are the questions the culture asks you as you prepare for marriage.

This kind of deception is just another strand in the web of lies that you have been told your whole life—that everything is about you. It's a deception and a manipulation of your heart, mind, soul, and body.

You have bigger and better hopes and dreams for your marriage than the culture does. And God has even bigger and better hopes and dreams for your marriage than you can imagine for yourself.

God's dream for your marriage is not me-centric. It is not a selfish dream. God dreams that your marriage will be a dynamic collaboration between you, your spouse, and him. He has plans for you and your future spouse, and he knows that those plans will lead you to an even greater happiness than you have planned for yourself.

This idea leads us to an odd paradox. Marriage is not about your wants and desires. In fact, the more you let go of your own plans and give them over to God, the happier you will be. Your life and your marriage will be better than you could have ever imagined.

Marriage is not 50-50 at all. In fact, it's more like 100-100, with each of you giving everything you have to the other. And then add in God on top of that.

Have you ever had a time when you discovered God's plans were better than your own? Maybe something didn't work out the way you'd planned. Perhaps it's a relationship that didn't last or a job you didn't get. At first, you feel disappointment because things didn't go your way. But soon you meet someone or discover an opportunity that ends up being even better than the relationship or job you had wanted in the first place.

Life is filled with ups and down and twists and turns. There will be so many times when things don't go how you think they will. Remembering the times when you learned God's plans were better than yours will help fill you with hope during those twists and turns. And that hope can make all the difference in a marriage.

God is going to surprise you a thousand times just like that in your marriage.

Discuss:

Discuss with your future husband or wife some times in your life when something didn't go as you had planned, but in the end things turned out even better than you had imagined.

....

....

....

....

....

....

....

....

....

....

....

....

....

....

....

....

....

....

....

Marriage is the most natural state of man ... the state in which you will find solid happiness.

— Benjamin Franklin

What It's Really About

Nothing is better than an experience that exceeds our expectations.

Think about it. You call a customer service line expecting a long wait to speak with a grumpy employee who doesn't care about you or the product they are representing. Instead you get a quick answer from a real, live person whose voice is filled with energy and enthusiasm, who cares about your experience and is pleasant in fulfilling your needs. Or you pull forward at the coffee shop drive-thru line only to find that the person in front of you paid for your coffee.

Little moments like these don't happen all the time, but when they do it's an instant game changer. Reality exceeds our expectations.

God's vision for marriage is kind of like that.

The culture has a very specific vision of marriage that is based on one emotion: fear. Fear of missing out. Fear that you will miss out on something better by getting married. The culture says marriage is too limiting. It takes away your time. It takes away your freedom. It takes away your self-expression. And if you have kids, then, the culture says, you will simply never have freedom, time, or pleasure again!

I hope your expectations of marriage exceed the culture's meager vision for marriage. But I guarantee you that God's vision for marriage far exceeds even your own expectations.

God has a big vision for your marriage. It's greater than anything we could dream up. It's based not on missing out, but on gaining something bigger and better.

God's vision of marriage will unfold before you in the years to come, as you enjoy the fruits of your life together, but it can be summed up in three words: faithful, lifelong, and life-giving.

God has a vision for marriage that is faithful. That a husband and wife would give themselves entirely to each other and only to each other. There is a beauty to faithfulness that can only be experienced for yourself. Faithful people keep their promises and enjoy the freedom of knowing they can really count on someone. What a gift!

God's vision is for a marriage that is lifelong. That a husband and wife would become one, and would not be separated until 'death do us part.' Very few things last a lifetime, but God created marriage to do just that. For better, for worse. How special!

And God has a vision for marriage that is life-giving. That you would seek to bring children into a loving home, that you would raise those children in love and in the faith that God loves them too. God creates life, and he invites us into that miracle of giving life too. Amazing!

Faithful, lifelong, life-giving. This is God's vision for your marriage. It certainly runs in stark contrast to the culture's vision for marriage. But just in case you think God's vision for marriage isn't bigger and better than the culture's vision, let me ask you a few jarring questions.

How would you feel if I told you that your spouse was going to cheat on you?

How would you feel if I told you that you would endure a messy divorce, and your children would always have to live with its painful aftereffects?

How would you feel if I told you, right now, that you would never have children?

It's painful to think about these scenarios. But they reveal a stark reality: Deep inside, we want exactly what God wants. We want a marriage that is faithful, lifelong, and life-giving. We don't really

Exercise:

What do you sense God saying to you in this section?

....

....

....

....

....

....

....

....

....

....

....

....

....

....

....

....

....

....

....

....

....

....

....

....

....

....

want the culture's vision. We want God's vision. We want the vision that is bigger and better than we ever imagined. When we embrace God's vision we aren't missing out; we're going for something far bigger and better.

Through your marriage you will discover parts of yourself that are far greater than you can imagine. Being a faithful person will open a dimension of you that inspires you and the people around you. In the same way, a lifelong relationship will give you freedom to explore parts of life unknown to everyone else.

You have a vision for your life and God has a vision for your life, but marriage helps you see that God's vision is far greater than yours. Marriage helps make his greater vision a reality.

Is God's vision demanding? Sure. A faithful, lifelong, life-giving marriage demands that we passionately strive to be the-best-version-of-ourselves. But as St. John Paul the Great said, "It is natural for the human heart to accept demands, even difficult ones, in the name of love for an ideal, and above all in the name of love for a person."

Pray to God and invite him to exceed your expectations for your marriage preparation experience. Invite him to help you exceed the expectations of your wife- or husband-to-be. And invite him to exceed your expectations for your marriage.

It is Jesus... that you seek when you dream of happiness; he is waiting for you when nothing else you find satisfies you... it is he who provokes you with that thirst for fullness that will not let you settle for compromise.

— St John Paul II

God's Dream for Marriage

1.1
1.2
1.3
1.4
1.5

No Regrets

Pray Together:

**Grant me, O Lord my God,
A mind to know you,
A heart to seek you,
Wisdom to find you,
Conduct pleasing to you,
Faithful perseverance in
waiting for you,
And a hope of finally
embracing you.**

Amen

—St. Thomas Aquinas

John felt like he needed just one more moment. He needed to stand here just a moment longer.

He stared down at the red rose under his hand, pressed against the cold metallic gray of the coffin. And he needed just one more moment.

Not far under his hand was the love of his life, his wife of fifty-six years. His beloved. Not far under his hand was the woman he had built his life with.

She was waiting for him when he got back from World War II. They built their home together, where they would raise five beautiful children. The home he still lived in today.

Not far under his hand was the woman he had been with in good times and in bad, in sickness and in health. The hand he had held so often it felt like a part of him. The face he had looked into so long that he knew it better than his own.

So John needed just one more moment before lifting his hand off the rose, leaning in close, kissing that cold gray metal, and whispering, "Goodbye, my love."

Then he turned around. His eyes drifted slowly over his five children and their spouses, who were all surrounding him. Behind them were his nineteen grandchildren, so many of them with their own husbands or wives. Surrounding them were his thirty-two great-grandchildren, the littlest ones crying in their mothers' arms. And still, beyond the family were friends, neighbors, coworkers, and members from their parish. John knew there were a lot more roses to be placed on that coffin. And looking out over the crowd of people who loved his wife, as he took his first step so others could say their final good-byes, John felt a profound sense of sadness, a loss beyond anything he had ever experienced. But he also had a deep sense of satisfaction, of a life well lived and well loved.

Someday, years from now, as you and your spouse sit on your back porch and watch the sunset for the ten thousandth time, as you hold each other's hands and think back over your lives together, God wants you to know the deep and peaceful satisfaction of having lived your marriage well.

God wants you to be able to look back and remember all the good that has come from your life together. He wants you to experience all the rewards of a life well lived and well loved. He wants you to reminisce about all the ways you grew and the good things you experienced that you never anticipated or foresaw.

Because there is an alternative. God doesn't want your heart filled with regret. He doesn't want you to know shame or disappointment many years from now. He doesn't want you to feel resentment or anger.

God has bigger things in store for you than that. He's got a greater dream for your marriage, a vision of a life well lived, a plan for a job well done. In the end, God wants to be able to say to you, "Well done, my good and faithful servant." There is nothing better than hearing those words.

So much is going to happen in your life. You have so many hopes and dreams for your marriage and for your future. But in the end, when you think of looking into your husband's eyes or holding your wife's hand, and you know you have lived life well, can you really imagine any better feeling?

I want to help you prepare for that kind of marriage. Thank you for letting me be a part of your journey. I'm praying for you.

May God bless you.

God has a big vision for your marriage.

___

Additional Resources

What the Church, the Bible, and the Saints Teach
Us About the Sacrament of Marriage

God is the Author of Marriage

Marriage is a beautiful thing, perhaps even more beautiful than we can imagine. Beautiful, loving, inspiring marriages are part of God's plan.

God made you and you are good. He made you in his image. Male and female he created you. And he made you to be joined together as one. You were made to be good for one another.

That's why God has brought you together. He has a dream for the two of you. He is the author of marriage.

———————————————

You were made to be good for one another.

1602 Sacred Scripture begins with the creation of man and woman in the image and likeness of God and concludes with a vision of "the wedding-feast of the Lamb." Scripture speaks throughout of marriage and its "mystery," its institution and the meaning God has given it, its origin and its end, its various realizations throughout the history of salvation, the difficulties arising from sin and its renewal "in the Lord" in the New Covenant of Christ and the Church.

The Lord God said, "It is not good for the man to be alone. I will make a suitable partner for him."
(Gen. 2:18)

Cast yourself upon God and have no fear.
—St. Augustine

Notes

A happy marriage is a long conversation
which always seems too short.

—André Maurois

What Are Your Dreams?

SESSION 2

Wisdom for Priorities from Helen and Joe

I collect stories about marriages. You never know where you are going to find good marriage wisdom. I actually found this wise story of Helen and Joe while reading the news.

When Helen Auer died on a Wednesday, she was sitting in her chair. Her husband of seventy-three years came into the room and knew right away. Joe leaned over, gave her a kiss goodbye, and whispered in her ear, "Helen, call me home."

Twenty-eight hours later, Helen did just that. Joe Auer died at the age of one hundred. His children figured he could manage one night without her, but not two. Not long afterward, the family had a funeral Mass in front of the same altar where Helen and Joe were married in 1941.

This couple met at church and had their first of ten children before Joe went off to fight in World War II. Helen was pregnant with their second when he left. She kissed him at the end of the driveway, and he walked toward the train terminal on his way to fight in the U.S. Army.

Helen was able to mail him a photo, somewhere in France, of her with their two children, Barry and Judy. Joe would meet Judy for the first time when she was three years old.

Joe carried that photo in his wallet as he trudged through Europe after landing at Utah Beach on D-Day. He kept it in his wallet, in fact, the rest of his life, smudged and worn and endlessly important. "It never left his wallet," Jerry Auer, Helen and Joe's tenth and youngest child, said. "It's still in there right now."

Mary Jo, one of their daughters, helped prepare the funeral. "It's a joyous time," she said. "Mom and Dad lived a blessed life." Mary Jo retired early so she could help her parents at the end, when Helen's arthritis was getting bad and Joe needed help with the meals and the laundry. She said her mother was the gregarious one. "She loved her family and her friends. She loved being busy with her family."

Joe was quieter and handled the discipline in the family. But Mary Jo said he was defined by his dedication to his faith and his family.

"Dad thought of his children as a gift from God. That was a responsibility for him," she said. "He taught us to be servants to God and to be caretakers of his earth. He was recycling on his last day."

Joe and Helen's marriage survived because they loved each other, they worked at it, and they shared a devout faith.

Money was a little tight and ten children can add stress to any relationship, but they always managed. Joe used to take two buses each way to his job as an engraver. He bought his first car when he retired.

When their youngest was in third grade, Helen went to work in the cafeteria at the

St. Lawrence Parish school making hot lunches. She and four other women would spend the whole morning chatting and singing. They were called "the sisters of the skillet."

Eventually the Auers had sixteen grandchildren, twenty-nine great-grandchildren, and one great-great-grandchild—all of whom have a marvelous example to live up to.

"They were simple, humble people. They wanted nothing and got everything in return," Jerry Auer said. "If somebody were thinking of getting married, they could do a lot worse than to look at my parents."

———————————

What Are Your Dreams?

2.1
2.2
2.3
2.4
2.5

Two Great Gifts

It's important to anticipate. Think about the last time you went on vacation. You planned for months, saved up, booked a hotel and maybe plane tickets. You sat down and planned out your itinerary. You researched the places you would go and things you would see. You anticipated and enjoyed every moment of that preparation. Then the trip finally came, and it felt like it flew by.

When you compare how much time you spend anticipating a trip with how much time you actually spend on the trip itself, you realize that anticipation is most of the fun of the whole experience! And this isn't just true of vacation. It's also true of your wedding day.

God invites us to be a people of anticipation. He wants us to be a people who look forward into the future and see a-better-version-of-ourselves, the best versions of our friends and family, and a better version of the world. God wants us to be a people who see a future that is bigger and better than the past.

But the problem is sometimes we waste our anticipation. We wish we could skip the waiting and just get to it.

Your wedding day is a perfect example. Right now, you are in a time of preparation and anticipation. First, there are all the logistics. The cake, the dress, the seating assignments, the venue, the honeymoon. And there is also the time of preparation for each of you as individuals, a time to prepare your hearts for your life together as husband and wife.

It's easy to wish this time away. How many mornings have you woken up and wished it was already your wedding day?

But your wedding day is going to be over so fast—in an instant. The day will be here and gone before you know it. The wise couple knows this and doesn't waste their anticipation. But how do you do that?

God invites you to see the future. That's how.

It doesn't matter if you are sixteen or sixty, the rest of your life is ahead of you. You can't change one moment of your past, but you can change your whole future.

What would the world be like without someone like Martin Luther King Jr., who dreamed of a better future? How many people could look into the future and see that Ichijirou Araya would climb Mount Fuji at one hundred years old? He was probably the only one who could see that dream. Or how many people could look at a flat stretch of land in New York City and envision the Empire State Building? What would the world be like without people who can look into the future and see things that no one else can see? People who can dream?

God invites you to look into the future and see something amazing. He wants you to work toward something amazing. And he has given us all two great gifts to help us do just that.

The first gift is our free will. We are all endowed with free will from the moment we are born. This gift means our choices are our own. We get to decide what our future will be like. We have the freedom to choose. Free will is a great gift that says the future is what we make of it.

Don't waste your power to choose. After all, one of the requirements of a valid marriage is that you are coming to it freely, that it is your choice. Free will is one of the most powerful tools for the life you hope to build.

The second gift is our ability to dream. When we dream, we look into the future, see the bigger and better reality, and then come back to the present and work to make that future a reality. This is one of God's greatest gifts to us. It's why anticipation means so much to us. When we anticipate and prepare, we are working to make the future we have dreamed of a reality.

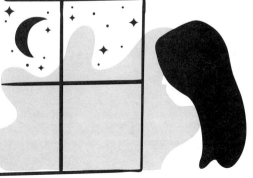

Free will and our ability to dream. Use them. Look into the future and imagine what kind of husband you want to be. Imagine what kind of mother you want to be. Imagine what kind of couple and family you want to be and create. Then come back to the present and use your free will to choose to make that future a reality.

Exercise:

Are you great at dreaming? Have you forgotten how? Think about some of your dreams as a child, such as what you wanted to be when you grew up. What kind of dreams do you have now? How good are you at anticipating and preparing? Talk to your future husband or wife about these questions and your ability to dream.

Love recognizes no barriers. It jumps hurdles, leaps fences, penetrates walls to arrive at its destination full of hope.

—Maya Angelou

What Are Your Dreams?

2.1
2.2
2.3
2.4
2.5

Your Dream List

What are your dreams?

This question is a part of the daily conversation at Dynamic Catholic. But many people have never before considered the question. What are your dreams?

Often when you ask people this question, their answers are vague and general, not thought out in any detail. Some people will even believe they do not have any dreams.

Either way, most people seem surprised by the question. But when we fail to dream, we waste God's gift of that ability. That's why it is important to dream, think about our dreams, and take steps to achieve them.

Only very rarely does someone say, "I want these things, for these reasons, and this is how I intend to achieve them. . . ." Without exception, these are the people who are living life passionately and enthusiastically. They very rarely complain. They don't talk negatively about others. You never hear them refer to happiness as some future event linked to retirement, marriage, a promotion, or some financial windfall.

So, what do these people have that most people don't? They know what they want.

Do you know what you want?

Most people can tell you exactly what they don't want, but very few have the same clarity about what they do want.

If you don't know what you want from life, everything will appear either as an obstacle or as a burden. But the whole world gets out of the way for people who know what they want and where they are going. Be assured, if you don't know where you are going, you are lost.

Here are ten categories of dreams to help spur your thoughts and get you started.

1. Adventure: If you could travel to any three places in the next ten years, where would you go?

2. Creative: What hobby or sport would you like to pursue?

3. Physical: What aspect of your physical health and wellness would you like to improve?

4. Legacy: What ministry, cause, or charity would you like to start supporting or increase your support for?

5. Emotional: What one relationship would you like to improve or grow?

6. Psychological: If you could suspend fear, what activity would you try?

7. Professional: What's your dream job?

8. Intellectual: If you could speak an additional language, what would it be?

9. Spiritual: What's your dream for how you might develop a greater sense of inner peace? Who does God want you to be?

10. Character: What character qualities do you notice in other people that you would like to expand in your own life?

For years the Dynamic Catholic team has been encouraging people to create dream lists. Your dream list serves as the foundation for the bigger vision you have for your life.

The truth is that when someone begins to think about dreams in the context of the ten categories, their dreams materialize rather quickly. Most people soon discover that it is not that they don't have dreams, but rather that they have so many dreams, they can't possibly pursue them all.

This is where God comes into the equation. The sheer number of our dreams is one of the reasons we pray: to ask God which dreams we should chase in our lives. He is the source of all our dreams. When we aren't sure what to do, it's always a good idea to go to the source.

This is a great point in your marriage preparation to stop and ask yourself: What are my dreams? This could be the most important moment of your marriage preparation. People who dream are simply more engaged in life. People who dream are more interesting. Period. And couples who learn to dream together have marriages that are longer, fuller, and happier. Now is your time to dream.

Exercise:

Spend ten minutes answering the question for yourself. **What are your dreams?** Begin a dream list and write them down.

Use the ten dream categories to give clarity to your process. There are no right or wrong answers. Write quickly; don't think too much. Don't analyze or edit yourself as you make your list. Write everything down, even the things you feel are foolish. Your answers don't have to be definitive; they will change over time. In fact, some of them will probably change by the time you finish marriage preparation. But it is still important to write them down now. It will help you as you venture through the rest of your life. So write your list, and when you are done, date it and share it with your future spouse.

Love Is Not About Compromise

We all have dreams. But most of us don't readily share them with others. "What if I look foolish?" "What if I fail?" Sharing your dreams might make you feel vulnerable to judgment or scrutiny. Whatever the reason, most of us just aren't aware of the dreams of the people in our lives. And this includes those closest to us.

God has given you dreams as an individual. You know this. But he has given your future husband or wife dreams too. And at some point both you and your future spouse are going to be called to sacrifice one of your individual dreams for the betterment of the marriage. This isn't a maybe. It's going to happen.

Sacrifice is a funny thing. We will sacrifice just about anything for ourselves and our own dreams. We will suffer the loss of sleep, the loss of time, the loss of money, and so much more for the pursuit of our own dreams. It's not so hard when you do it for yourself. Why? Because we love ourselves.

But what about when your love for your wife means you have to put yourself second? What happens when you have to put your own dreams on hold?

My husband and I started dating in college, and we would share our dreams and goals with each other. Once we got engaged, we started building our dreams together. After college, Andy was accepted into a wonderful graduate program. When we got married a year later, that meant a new city, new place to live, and putting some dreams and plans in motion and adjusting others or putting them on hold.

The question is, what do you love?

You can choose not to love the right things, but you cannot choose not to love. It's what we were created for. You tell me what you love and I will tell you who you are. What you fall in love with determines everything.

Because you so deeply love your spouse, you can bet there will be times in your marriage when you must sacrifice what you want for him or her. It comes with the territory. And that's OK. In fact, it's a good thing.

Two people helping each other achieve their dreams creates incredible intimacy. Dreaming and sacrifice live at the center of that. That's one of the reasons you're getting married, right? Because you believe the future can be bigger than the past.

I've been married for 13 years, and I can tell you with absolute certainty that dreaming together, setting goals, making plans, sacrificing for each other, cheering each other on, and most importantly, making your spouse's dreams your dreams and vice-versa. This will take sacrifice, but it will also become your greatest adventure. True love unites minds and hearts: two sets of dreams become one great dream.

Sacrificing for each other's dreams requires intimacy. And it's a beautiful thing.

To hear more wisdom from our contributors, go to **DynamicCatholic.com/ViewProgram**

Exercise:

Name ten of your partner's dreams. Take turns and name each other's dreams. See if you can get to ten. Don't be worried if you can't. That's OK. Don't feel guilty or feel like you aren't a good couple. Use this exercise as an incredible opportunity. It's the start of a wonderful conversation that will never end. Your marriage gives you a partner to dream with.

....
....
....
....
....
....
....
....
....
....
....
....
....
....
....
....
....

This is the secret of life: the self lives only by dying, finds its identity (and its happiness) only by self-forgetfulness, self-giving, self-sacrifice, and agape love.

—Peter Kreeft

What Are Your Dreams?

A Crucial Habit

Life is about dreams and decisions. You dream the dreams and you make the decisions. From an infinite number of possibilities you will decide how to spend your life.

How do you make your decisions?

What is different about the way couples with great marriages make decisions? A number of things, but right now I want to focus on just one:

They allow themselves to dream together.

Most people base their decisions on the limited resources available to them at the present moment. But couples in great marriages place no limitations upon their decision-making process. They ask: What would be best? What does God hope for us? If we could do anything, what would we do?

These husbands and wives who experience a healthy marriage remove limitations from their dreams. They are not guided by fear, anger, greed, or lust. Once they establish their dreams, they seek them with unrelenting energy.

So let me ask: What are your dreams for your marriage? What do you want your marriage to look like? What do you want it to be known for? Maybe your dreams look something like this:

- Having someone who really understands me.
- Having someone who I can talk to about anything.
- Like John in the story from Session 1, I dream of creating a family that will produce dozens of great-grandchildren one day.
- Having someone who is in my corner, on my side, all the time.
- Starting a family and being foster parents.
- Having someone to run a marathon with.
- Being known for taking risks and adventures.
- Having someone to take care of me when I need it.
- Buying a house together and building a life.

- Creating and sharing holiday traditions.
- Having someone to come home to.
- Growing old together.

These dreams are all valid and serve as a great start to your life of dreaming together. You have dreams now, and as you move forward they will change and evolve. Sometimes they will become very specific dreams: taking a dream vacation. Other times they will be great ideals: raising children who are happy, healthy, and holy.

Making dreams a regular part of your conversation as a married couple is a crucial habit for your marriage. Two people pursuing a dream together and helping each other achieve their own dreams creates a deep intimacy. The benefits for your marriage of dreaming won't just be the amazing things you achieve. It will also breed a level of communication, trust, excitement, and affection that many couples lack.

To make this simple, let me give you a recommendation: **Always have at least one dream you are working toward as a couple.** It doesn't always have to be something complex or life altering. It is good for us to have simple dreams too. Perhaps you could work toward a dream of learning new recipes to cook together, or reading ten books each in the next year. Other times your dreams will be bigger. You could work together toward that mission trip to Haiti you have always wanted to take, or buying your dream home. Or work together toward the dream of paying off student loans.

It doesn't matter if it's a big dream or a simple dream; always have at least one you are working toward. It will draw you closer as a couple, teach you how to plan and relate to each other, and help you learn how to overcome setbacks. It will also prepare you for life in a way nothing else can.

49

Exercise:

Dream together. You don't have to get everything down right now. This is just the start of your life of dreaming. It can help to use time as a structure.

What are three five-year dreams you have for your marriage?

How about three ten-year dreams?

Three twenty-five-year dreams?

What are three fifty-year dreams you have for your marriage?

Imagine what it will be like to look into each other's eyes at seventy, eighty, ninety years old. What kind of person do you want to be for your wife? What kind of woman do you want your husband to see? When you look back at your life when you're ninety, what do you hope you will remember?

You know you're in love when you can't fall asleep because reality is finally better than your dreams.

—Dr. Seuss

What Are Your Dreams?

Red Flags

Reflect:

Consider these words about God and how they reflect your dreams for your marriage.

Nothing is more practical than finding God, than falling in Love in a quite absolute, final way.

What you are in love with, what seizes your imagination, will affect everything.

It will decide what will get you out of bed in the morning, what you do with your evenings, how you spend your weekends, what you read, whom you know, what breaks your heart, and what amazes you with joy and gratitude.

Fall in Love, stay in love, and it will decide everything.

—Fr. Pedro Arrupe, SJ

The heartbeat of the mission at Dynamic Catholic is to help people become the-best-version-of-themselves. **That means knowing the distinction between thriving and just surviving.**

There are some things we need simply to survive. Examples of these would be food and water, and air to breathe.

But there are other needs that are not critical to our survival. This second group of needs helps us not merely to survive but to thrive. We can survive without them for years in many cases. But they are essential if we are going to thrive. When these needs are being fulfilled, we begin to blossom as human beings. Among these needs are regular exercise, a healthy and balanced diet, and loving and healthy relationships.

If you are married, you will not be able to thrive as an individual if you are not thriving in your marriage. It's just not possible. And like all areas that are necessary to thrive, some activities are critical and others aren't.

It is not absolutely critical that you go to dinner and the movies once a month. But it is critical to a thriving marriage that you continue to spend special time with your mate. It is essential that you spend special time together, but it is not absolutely critical that you spend it in one specific way or another.

Like sleep, dreaming isn't just a good idea for your marriage. It is absolutely necessary for it to survive and thrive. Why? Consider this: if everything was built by people who believed the future can be bigger and better than the past, then the opposite is also true. When you stop believing that the future will be bigger and better than the past, you are in real trouble.

Dreaming creates an endless canvas for you to paint your life upon. Will you start a business together? Will you build your dream home on a lake? Will you serve the teenagers at your parish to help build their dreams?

But when you stop dreaming, you stop envisioning a future altogether.

If you can't dream together, your marriage is in trouble, plain and simple. Failing to dream together is a huge red flag for your marriage. When you see it, it's time to do something about it.

I want you to get really clear on this. If you find yourself failing to envision a future together, it's time to do something that very moment. Schedule time that week to discuss your dreams and why you have been struggling to envision your future. Have an honest conversation about next steps and whether you might need to get someone to help you, whether it is a mentor couple, a marriage coach, your priest, or a counselor.

Too often people wait for one or two or three more red flags, and by then it might be too late. In many cases by the time things are bad enough that they are actually addressed out in the open, it's just too late. Most marriage counselors will tell you that couples usually wait until it is way too late before asking for help. Remember how this journey began in the very first session: Honesty will be your best friend in your marriage.

Envision your future together, a future that is bigger and better than now. Dream together. It's incredibly satisfying to achieve a dream, but there is nothing quite like sharing a dream with each other, articulating it clearly, and chasing it together. It's a powerful part of marriage.

Life is about dreams and decisions.

___

What Are Your Dreams?

Additional Resources

What the Church, the Bible, and the Saints Teach
Us About the Sacrament of Marriage

Free Will and Consent

Life is choices. When you marry, you are choosing this sacrament of your own free will. You give your entire self and your consent to your spouse in the vows. When you and your spouse say, "I do," you want to say and hear those words with no reservations. Without consent, there is no marriage.

From your consent and from your sexual consummation of marriage, a special bond emerges between husband and wife. This bond is lifelong and exclusive. The marriage bond has been established by God, so it cannot be dissolved.

That's why the Church wants you to be fully prepared to receive this sacrament.

———————————

CATECHISM

1626 The Church holds the exchange of consent between the spouses to be the indispensable element that "makes the marriage." If consent is lacking there is no marriage.

1627 The consent consists in a "human act by which the partners mutually give themselves to each other": "I take you to be my wife"—"I take you to be my husband." This consent that binds the spouses to each other finds its fulfillment in the two "becoming one flesh."

1628 The consent must be an act of the will of each of the contracting parties, free of coercion or grave external fear. No human power can substitute for this consent. If this freedom is lacking the marriage is invalid.

1731 Freedom is the power, rooted in reason and will, to act or not to act, to do this or that, and so to perform deliberate actions on one's own responsibility. By free will one shapes one's own life. Human freedom is a force for growth and maturity in truth and goodness; it attains its perfection when directed toward God, our beatitude.

SCRIPTURE

Whatever you do, do it all in the name of the Lord Jesus.
(Colossians 3:17)

SAINT

Love to be real, it must cost. . . it must empty us of self.
—St. Teresa of Calcutta

Notes

The Expe Gap

All, everything that I understand,

I understand only because I love.

—Leo Tolstoy

The Expectations Gap

SESSION 3

Wisdom for the Future from Ron and Vicky

I met Ron and Vicky right before they got married, when I helped them in their preparation for marriage. Neither of them had had an easy journey in life. They each had suffered and struggled in particularly painful ways. But now, both of them were taking this coming marriage very seriously; they knew God had a dream for their life together. And they were eager to overcome the pain of their pasts and pursue this dream together.

For Ron and Vicky, the challenges came not from being too dependent on parents and family. Quite the opposite: Neither of them had any real family to learn from or to provide a base of stability and love. As we did their marriage preparation together, we discussed family history and what each of them would be bringing to the marriage. Studies show that most couples tend to create the kind of marriage and family they have seen and grown up in as children.

This was a concern for Ron. He shared that his mother had been married three times and he had never met his father. He told of his own divorce in his first marriage and the damage it caused his two children. Ron felt alone in the world. His childhood family of origin had been chaotic. In fact, he would say that he really had no family at all. When I asked him about the habits he would be bringing to the marriage from his background in the Wilson family, he simply said, "I am the Wilson family." In other words, he was completely on his own.

When he looked behind him, his past was riddled with nothing but abandonment, pain, and instability. He was starting over in this marriage from scratch.

He hoped to bring none of the habits he had learned from his family of origin.

Ron deeply desired to pursue God's dream for marriage. He hoped for a future bigger than his past, and he knew it was not going to be easy for him. He yearned to have a loving, healthy relationship with his wife, yet he had experienced brokenness and disappointment in every familial relationship he'd ever had. For him, his family of origin would not be meddling in his new marriage; rather, they would be completely absent except in the pain they had left behind in his life.

For Ron, a dynamic marriage would be a new concept. He would need to create new habits in order to learn how to love his new wife, Vicky, in a healthy way. He knew for sure what he did not want in his marriage and life; he was just beginning the journey to discover what he did want. Breaking that cycle of a painful past would require unlearning many old habits and acquiring new ones to build the future he so deeply desired.

Patience enables you to endure change.

The Expectations Gap

3.1
3.2
3.3
3.4
3.5

Disappointment, Resentment, Anger, Frustration, and Loss of Trust

When my wife asks what time I will be home tonight and I tell her six o'clock, I've just created an expectation. She expects me to be home by six o'clock.

Once I have created that expectation, I have only three options:
1. Meet it: Be home at six.
2. Disappoint it: Show up later, without letting her know.
3. Manage it: Communicate clearly what is going on and whether I will be able to be home by six.

The truth is, by two in the afternoon, I pretty much know how my day is going. And I also have a very good idea of whether I will actually be able to be home by six.

A smart guy, facing challenges at two p.m., calls and says, "I'm still at work; I'm facing some issues here. I'm unfortunately not going to be home at six." He is managing the expectation.

His wife is also smart, so she asks, "OK, when will you be home?" She is managing back and resetting the expectation.

The husband says, "It's looking like eight o'clock." He doesn't really think he can make it by eight, but he is really, really hoping to make it happen. He is an optimist and he wants to make it home even though deep down he knows it is unlikely to happen.

What is he doing by saying this? He has disappointed the first expectation, and he is setting himself up to do it all over again. **We create an "expectations gap" when we fail to live up to the expectation someone has for us.** That's the space between the expectation itself and the reality of the unmet expectation.

What the husband should do instead is say, "I'd be guessing if I told you right now. Let me text you an update later. And I will call as soon as I get in the car, so you'll know for sure. OK?" That would be managing the expectation, communicating clearly, and being helpful.

Of course, he does have one other option. He could never call at all. Then he could walk in at eight forty-five and find his wife filled with disappointment, resentment, anger, frustration, and loss of trust.

Because that is what fills the gap of unmet expectations: disappointment, resentment, anger, frustration, and loss of trust.

The same thing is true for products you buy. A powder promises that it will clean something, but it doesn't actually do it. The product sets an expectation and then fails to live up to it; it disappoints. Trust is lost.

When a product does that, it kills its brand. You don't trust that brand because it does not meet expectations. Reality fails to meet the expectation. The brand fails to keep its promises.

It may seem like a small thing, but good brands keep their promises. They depend on trust. No trust, no purchase. No purchase, no relationship.

And the same thing is true with relationships and marriages. They rise and fall based on trust. Too much disappointment, resentment, anger, frustration, and loss of trust and eventually the relationship falls apart from the inside out, because there's no trust.

My son loves to go fishing with me. I'm his daddy. And he likes to write "Go fishing with Daddy" on dates all over the calendar on his wall. At first, he would be disappointed when I did not show up to go fishing on the days he had scheduled it. Finally, I had to sit him down and say, "Son, when you write down 'Go fishing with Daddy,' you have to let me know about that too. I have to put it on my calendar also. Otherwise, I have no idea that you are planning on that."

We need our expectations to match up.

Exercise:

Can you think of a time when you expected someone to do or say something and they failed to do so? Do you think the expectations were clear on their end too?

_____

_____

_____

_____

_____

_____

_____

_____

_____

_____

_____

_____

_____

_____

_____

_____

_____

_____

_____

_____

_____

_____

_____

_____

Do not think that love, in order to be genuine, has to be extraordinary. What we need is to love without getting tired.

—St. Teresa of Calcutta

The Expectations Gap

3.1
3.2
3.3
3.4
3.5

Everybody Has Expectations About Everything

Everybody has expectations about everything. And we all certainly have expectations for our spouse. Being clear about those expectations and being honest with each other builds trust. When our spouse has no idea what we expect, they cannot possibly meet those expectations. After all, the hardest expectations to meet are the ones you don't know about.

And we all have expectations.

For example, Susan might say, "I expect my husband to be my best friend. That's why I married him. That deep friendship means everything to me. His personality just makes me feel good. I love that about him. We can laugh together. I have so many warm feelings when I think of all the fun stuff we do and how much I enjoy being with him. I can really be myself when I am around him. My hope is that we can have a date night at least once a week even when we have kids. That together time is really important to me. I have an expectation of regular time together and a weekly date night."

William would say, "I expect my wife to want a large family like I do. I grew up in a big family; I've got a bunch of brothers and cousins and everything. I really want that, and she should want that too. I mean, who doesn't love kids? And family? Especially my family. We are really a lot of fun, and my hope is that she will love being a part of everything we do together. I have an expectation of our own large family, and I expect her to want to be a part of my extended family as well."

For example, Katie might say, "Rather than having big emotional arguments, I would like my husband to sit down with me and have a very civil, kind conversation so we can explore what we are disagreeing about. I expect him to treat me with respect and dignity, not to try to bully me or force me to cave in to whatever he wants. Like when we were trying to decide whether to spend five hundred dollars on a big-screen TV. There really was no need to get loud and defensive about the fact that I would rather spend that money on a couch. At least he told me what he thought instead of withdrawing and pouting, but I really expect him to be calm and reasonable when we disagree. I have an expectation of fair conversations when conflict occurs."

Charlie would say, "I expect that my wife will pay the bills and handle the finances. I don't like managing money, and my dad didn't either. My mom did a great job with that and was really good at making sure we stayed on budget. She always saved so that my dad did not feel pressure, even though they did like to argue about his boat and how much money he always wanted to spend (or waste) on it. I don't like credit cards either. On these kinds of practical things, I really would like my wife to be good at managing money."

There are a lot of areas where we have expectations of each other—how we will treat each other, how we will show affection and intimacy, practical things like money and family, lifestyle decisions, how we will handle old habits or past disappointments, how we will manage conflict and communicate, and what role faith will play in our life together.

What do you expect of your spouse? Expectations are good. We all have them. But the key to expectations is to be aware of them, to communicate them honestly, and to manage them together.

After all, the hardest expectations to meet are the ones you don't know about.

Exercise:

Write down one expectation you have of your future husband or wife in each of these areas:

1. How you will treat each other
2. What your family will look like
3. How you will practice your faith
4. How you will interact with each other's families during the holidays

....
....
....
....
....
....
....
....
....
....
....
....
....
....
....
....
....
....
....
....
....
....
....

Lord, grant that I might not so much seek to be loved as to love.

—St. Francis of Assisi

The Expectations Gap

3.1

3.2

3.3

3.4

3.5

What Do You Think Your Spouse Expects from You?

Expectations run both ways. It's easy to forget that. I am very clear in my mind as to what I expect of my wife. But it is easy for me to forget to consider what she expects of me. And sometimes I don't even know what she expects.

When Tony and Maria got married, Maria wanted to have several children as soon as they could. And she hoped to leave her full-time job as an accountant and be a stay-at-home mom once their second or third child was born. Since children and being a parent were very important to her, she assumed that Tony wanted the same things. So they didn't ever really discuss the details of family. They both wanted children, and they figured the rest would take care of itself.

After their second daughter was born, Maria told Tony it was time for her to stay home and be a full-time mother. Tony flew into a rage. "What are you talking about? We can't afford for you not to work. I don't make enough money for us to have a good life without you working too. Why are you just now sharing this with me?"

Maria had an expectation of Tony that he never knew about. Neither of them had ever thought to discuss the details of their family until the children began to arrive. Tony failed to meet Maria's expectations, and he was hurt. He felt like a failure when he realized that she hoped for something he did not feel like he could do. It also had never occurred to Tony to think about family from Maria's perspective. He had his own expectations that he wanted Maria to meet, but he did not have the awareness to realize that she had expectations in this area too. She had not brought up her hopes, and Tony had never asked.

When someone has an expectation that goes unmet, an expectations gap is created. And what fills the expectations gap? Disappointment, resentment, anger, frustration, and loss of trust.

Awareness that your spouse has expectations of you can prevent the pain that expectations gaps create.

What do you think your future husband or wife expects of you? Being able to answer that requires awareness.

When it comes to your friendship, do you think your fiancée expects you to be her best friend? How often do you think she would like the two of you to have a date once you are married? What is your plan for nurturing your relationship in the years to come to keep that friendship strong?

When it comes to conflict, how do you think your future wife would like you to speak, act, and treat her in moments when you disagree? Do you think she expects you to be passive, emotional, cool, or rational?

In the area of family, how many children do you think your husband-to-be hopes to have? How do you think he expects the two of you will raise your family? How do you think he will expect you to interact with his family and vice versa?

Finances can be challenging. Money usually is the source of the largest number of conflicts in a marriage. What might your future husband expect of you in this area when it comes to making, saving, spending, borrowing, and giving money to help other people?

There are a lot of areas where we have expectations of each other.

Expectations are good. We all have them. But the key to expectations is to be aware of them, to communicate them honestly, and to manage them together. And of course, sometimes that will require sacrifice.

Awareness of what your spouse expects of you can prevent the pain and loss of trust that failing to meet expectations can bring.

After all, the hardest expectations to meet are the ones you don't know about. What does your spouse expect of you?

Exercise:

Do the BETTER TOGETHER marriage inventory together.

DynamicCatholic.com/Inventory

Expectations
are good. We
all have them.

The Expectations Gap

3.1

3.2

3.3

3.4

3.5

Building on Your Strengths

We operate best when we play to our strengths. No one wants to build a career based on doing something they are not good at or that they hate doing. At the same time, your job or career will always have parts of it that you enjoy less or prefer to avoid. But you have to deal with those less desirable areas too. Knowing and using your key strengths can help you do just that.

In fact, doing what we are best at can usually help us compensate for what we are not so good at. And the same thing is true for marriages and relationships.

The BETTER TOGETHER marriage inventory shows you the areas of your relationship where you are strongest as a couple. Those are your strengths to build on.

The inventory also helps you discover the areas where you have the largest gaps in your relationship. These are the areas where you will need to have a plan to help you navigate together and prevent frustration.

The inventory is not a "compatibility score"; rather, it is designed to help you learn to understand and manage each other's expectations well. Every relationship has strengths and areas where we complement each other. And every relationship has areas where we don't have as much in common or where we view life differently.

Building on your strengths as a couple will help you navigate the more challenging areas of your relationship. All couples have unresolved conflicts in which they learn how to approach their differences in healthy ways.

After doing the BETTER TOGETHER inventory, Julie and John realized in a clearer way that their three areas of greatest strength were:

1. their deep friendship and affection for each other,
2. their shared love for their Catholic faith, and
3. the fact that they are both very flexible people, open and willing to change.

Love is the most necessary of all virtues.

—St. Anthony Mary Claret

The inventory also helped Julie and John to discover that the three areas where they had the biggest gaps to bridge were:

1. John's tendency to be more passive and avoid conflict at all costs, while Julie was much more emotionally expressive about areas of conflict,
2. their frequent disagreements about money and spending habits, and
3. their very different feelings about each other's families.

In discussing the BETTER TOGETHER inventory and what they'd learned, Julie and John decided on a good first step to begin to manage the conflicts inevitable in every marriage. They decided to apply their strengths to help bridge the gap in how they managed arguments and conflict.

Normally, John would avoid ever bringing up any disagreements. He would shut down when Julie began to get emotional about something they disagreed on. So they decided to begin to use their three greatest strengths to help in this area of how they managed conflict.

From now on, when they disagreed, they would choose first to remind themselves of their deep friendship by saying, "I know you love me and want what's best for me and for us." Julie would usually need to be the first to say this because John would go to any length to avoid the conflict and wouldn't say anything at all. But they agreed that when one said it, the other would say the same thing. This simple act would refocus the conflict on the knowledge that they both really loved each other and wanted what they thought was best for their marriage.

Then they would choose to leverage their love for the Catholic faith by simply saying a short prayer or the Our Father together. That way, they would be inviting a power greater than themselves into the conflict and discussion. Doing this also would help soften the moment and allow them to ease into a conversation about what they were disagreeing on.

Using these two strengths did not solve everything about their conflicts and arguments. But it did provide a starting point for remembering that their friendship and faith could help them navigate through those arguments in a more helpful way. They still disagreed about money and about their families. But deep friendship reminders and a simple prayer together gave them a first step toward navigating disagreements every marriage will face.

And when it comes to managing conflict, every relationship needs a first step.

Exercise:

What are the three things that surprised you most in doing the BETTER TOGETHER inventory? What did you learn that you didn't realize before?

The Expectations Gap

3.1

3.2

3.3

3.4

3.5

Expectations Change

Healthy people love to learn. Healthy people change and grow.

That is a beautiful part of what makes us human. We have the capacity to change and to grow; God made us that way.

As you have new experiences, your ideas, opinions, and beliefs change. It's true for all of us—you, me, and your spouse. Some old beliefs fade away. Some opinions get stronger and deeper. Some new ideas emerge and take root in your life.

When Mark was younger, he did not really have faith in God. He wasn't even sure God existed. When his father died, at the funeral Mass, Mark discovered a whole new faith in God the Father as he listened to the words about love and eternal life. His faith took root. It deepened. Now his faith plays an important role in everything he does.

Ten years ago, Suzanne never gave abortion a second thought. It seemed a like a bad idea, but it was really not something she dwelled on. But when she saw the ultrasound of her first child and then suffered a miscarriage a month later, her beliefs and ideas shifted. Now she sees the horror and tragedy of ending the life of an unborn child. She changed.

Joseph used to think poor people were poor because they made bad choices. He felt no need to help beggars or people living in tough situations. Their problems were their problems, not his. Until his company laid off one hundred workers, including him, and he needed help. His family, his friends, and his parish generously assisted him. And his views began to shift. Experience taught him new things.

Life happens. Education occurs. Your ideas and beliefs will grow and change. And your marriage will need to find ways to adapt and change with those. If both husband and wife are constantly growing, you will need to pay attention so that you grow together rather than apart.

And expectations can change over time. Lots of things can cause the expectations gap to widen or to shrink. Your wife may get a more demanding job, and that will change the dynamic of who does what in your relationship. You may have an autistic child, and your expectations will immediately shift in terms of who pitches in and when.

Life events happen. And when they do, it will impact your expectations of each other. Often we lock our spouse into something they said when we were dating. We think they won't change. We think, "She believes this, and that's that." Or "He'll never do that, and that's just the way it is." But you can't freeze it or lock it down, because the minute you do, something will change.

Change will come. So how do you stay alert and keep your relationship fresh and growing as the two of you grow and change individually?

When John and Amelia Rocchio celebrated their eighty-second wedding anniversary, he was 101; she was ninety-nine. Their anniversary made them the longest-married couple in America. Asked what the secret to their longevity was, John answered, "Patience."

In that single word, John captured the secret to changing expectations. Imagine all the changes their relationship had been through after eighty-two years of marriage.

It is tempting not to pay attention to the changes occurring in your spouse's life and priorities over time. After all, there are a lot of other areas of life that will require your attention, such as daily survival and the routines of work, home, children, and finances.

It is even more tempting to pay attention only to the life changes you yourself are experiencing.

Being patient with your husband day after day is not a natural human thing to do. Being patient with your wife as

SERENITY PRAYER

God grant me the serenity to accept the things I cannot change; courage to change the things I can; and wisdom to know the difference.

Amen.

she changes in small ways or large requires a lot. You cannot do these things without the Spirit of God assisting you. However, with the Spirit, you will grow more patient with all of the people in your life. Because God is patient.

Growing and changing with your spouse requires two things: **patience and communication.**

Patience enables you to endure change. In fact, it allows you to thrive through change because you know that your spouse is always changing and your relationship is always evolving. The changes of marriage become something you anticipate rather than dread. Patience helps you look eagerly ahead to what God will do next rather than resenting that your husband has added a few pounds or your wife no longer likes to go camping.

Communication is the first cousin of patience. The coming sessions will discuss active listening more. But when that listening occurs, you will quickly discover that you know firsthand how your mate is feeling, growing, and changing. Surprises will occur less frequently because you will know your partner well and see those changes coming. And when you know and can anticipate change, patience becomes much easier.

_____

Patience enables you to endure change.

Additional Resources

What the Church, the Bible, and the Saints Teach
Us About the Sacrament of Marriage

Men and Women Were Made for Each Other

God intended man and woman for each other from the very beginning. He created us in love for love. God knows you intimately because he created you.

Marriage is the intimate union and equal partnership of a man and a woman. It comes to us from the hand of God, who created male and female in his image, so that they might become one body and might be fruitful and multiply.

Men and women are equal as God's children, but they are created with important differences that allow them to give themselves and to receive the other as a gift.

CATECHISM

1604 For man is created in the image and likeness of God who is himself love. Since God created him man and woman, their mutual love becomes an image of the absolute and unfailing love with which God loves man.

SCRIPTURE

Then the Lord God said, "It is not good that the man should be alone; I will make him a helper as his partner." So out of the ground the Lord God formed every animal of the field and every bird of the air, and brought them to the man to see what he would call them; and whatever the man called every living creature, that was its name. The man gave names to all cattle, and to the birds of the air, and to every animal of the field; but for the man there was not found a helper as his partner. So the Lord God caused a deep sleep to fall upon the man, and he slept; then he took one of his ribs and closed up its place with flesh. And the rib that the Lord God had taken from the man he made into a woman and brought her to the man. Then the man said, "This at last is bone of my bones and flesh of my flesh; this one shall be called Woman, for out of Man this one was taken." Therefore a man leaves his father and his mother and clings to his wife, and they become one flesh. And the man and his wife were both naked, and were not ashamed.

(Genesis 2:18–25)

SAINT

The creation of woman is thus marked from the outset by the *principle of help*: a help which is not one-sided but *mutual*. Woman complements man, just as man complements woman: men and women are *complementary*. Womanhood expresses the "human" as much as manhood does, but in a different and complementary way. . . It is only through the duality of the "masculine" and the "feminine" that the "human" finds full realization.

—St. John Paul II, "Letter to Women"

Notes

Do we know how to say thank you? In your relationship [as husband and wife] it is important to keep alive your awareness that the other person is a gift from God, and we should always give thanks for gifts from God.

—Pope Francis

Seven Levels
of Intimacy

SESSION 4

Wisdom for Living Well from David and Sarah

When I read Matthew Kelly's *The Seven Levels of Intimacy* for the first time, I was delighted to meet David and Sarah in the opening story. They have inspired my marriage with wisdom ever since.

David Anderson lived in Boston with his wife, Sarah, and their three children, Rachel, Shannon, and Jonah. He was a very successful businessman, and one of the rewards of his success was their summer home on Martha's Vineyard. Sarah and the kids spent the whole summer there, while David usually spent part of each weekend and always came for the first two weeks in July.

One summer a few years ago, he made a promise to himself as he was driving out to the beach at the beginning of July. For two weeks, he was going to be a loving and attentive husband and father. He would make himself totally available. He would turn off his cell phone, resist the temptation to be constantly checking his email, and make himself completely available to his family and a genuine experience of vacation.

You see, David worked too much. He knew it. Everyone around him knew it. When you love your work, that's one of the dangers. When you rely on your work too much for your identity, that's one of the pitfalls. From time to time, David felt guilty about how much he worked, but he managed to brush the guilt aside by making the excuse that it was necessary. Sometimes he overcame his feelings of guilt by calling to mind the many privileges and opportunities that his wife and children were able to enjoy because he worked so hard.

Did the rationalizations work? Only temporarily. But this vacation was going to be different. David was going to be attentive and available.

The idea had come to him in his car, as he listened to a CD that a friend had given him. People were always giving him books to read and CDs to listen to, and the gifts always made him cringe, because he knew the giver would ask his opinion the next time their paths crossed—but for some reason, he had popped this CD in as he drove out of his garage that day.

The speaker was discussing dynamic relationships. Feeling a little uncomfortable, David was about to turn it off when something the man said struck him: "Love is a choice. Love is an act of the will. You can choose to love."

At that moment, David admitted to himself that as a husband he had been selfish, and that the love between him and Sarah had been dulled by his selfishness, by his insensitivity, by his unavailability. This self-centeredness manifested itself mostly in small ways. He insisted they watch whatever he wanted to watch on television. He made Sarah feel small for always being late. He constantly put his work before the needs of his family. He would take newspapers to work knowing that Sarah wanted to read them, and that he would be unlikely to have time to do so during his busy day. He was constantly saying, "Some other time," to his children, "Not now," to his wife. But for two weeks all that was going to change. And so it did.

From the moment David walked through the door, kissed his wife, and said, "You look really good in that sweater. That's a great color for you," Sarah was taken aback, surprised, even a little perplexed. Her first reaction was to wonder if he was having a dig at her for buying more clothes, but when he smiled and asked her, "What have I missed?" the genuine compliment settled in and felt wonderful.

After battling the traffic to get to the vacation house, David just wanted to sit down and relax, but Sarah suggested a walk on the beach. He began to refuse, but then thought better of it: "Sarah has been here all week long with the children, and now she just wants to be alone with me." So they walked on the beach hand in hand, while the children flew their kites.

The next morning, Sarah almost fell out of bed when David brought her breakfast. Admittedly, he had woken their daughter Rachel to help him pull that one off, but it was extraordinary nonetheless. Over breakfast he told her about a dream he'd had the night before, and then he asked, "What would you like to do today?"

Sarah couldn't remember the last time he had asked her that.

"Don't you have work to do?" she countered.

"No," he said. "We can do anything you want."

Over and over throughout the day David said to himself, "Love is a choice."

And so it went, for two weeks, without the constant harassment of cell phone calls and email. They visited the maritime museum, even though David hated museums; he allowed the kids to eat ice cream whenever they wanted; he even managed to hold his tongue when Sarah's getting ready made them late for his best friend's birthday dinner.

"Did Dad win something?" their daughter asked her mother one day. Sarah laughed, but she had been wondering herself what had come over her husband.

After lunch on the last day, David excused himself and walked the beach alone. He thought about the promise he had made to himself driving out two weeks earlier, and now made a new promise to keep choosing love when they got home.

That night as he and Sarah were preparing for bed, she suddenly stopped and looked at David with the saddest expression he'd ever seen on her face.

David panicked. "What's the matter?"

"Do you know something I don't know?" she asked.

"What do you mean?"

"The checkup I had a few weeks ago," Sarah said. "Did Dr. Lewis tell you something about me? Dave, you've been so good to me. Am I dying?"

David's eyes filled with tears. Wrapping her in his arms and holding her tight, he said, "No, honey. You're not dying. I'm just starting to live!"

———————

To be known and to know – that's what intimacy is.

___

Seven Levels of Intimacy

Clichés, Facts, and Opinions

What is intimacy?

First off, let's start with what intimacy is not. Intimacy is not sex. Sex doesn't guarantee intimacy, it is not required for intimacy, and intimacy doesn't belong to sex.

Intimacy is self-revelation. It's me revealing myself to you, and you revealing yourself to me. To be known and to know—that's what intimacy is.

So many times, instead of revealing ourselves and building intimacy, we hide ourselves. We spend a lot of our time and energy hiding ourselves away. Why? Because we are afraid. We are afraid that if people really knew us they wouldn't love us anymore. When someone tells us they love us we think, "You only love the person you think I am," or "You say that now, but if you really knew me you wouldn't love me anymore." This only leads to the opposite of intimacy: loneliness.

Can you think of anything lonelier than passing through life without ever being really known? You can be in a crowd and be lonely. You can be in a relationship and be lonely. Even someone we think is doing great can be lonely on the inside because they aren't known. People aren't lonely because they want to be. People are lonely because they don't know how to reveal themselves, or they don't have the opportunity to reveal themselves. The seven levels of intimacy are about learning how to give each other the opportunity to reveal yourself, and equipping you to do it.

On a very practical level, the seven levels of intimacy are about communication. How do we communicate with the lives we touch on a daily basis? How will you communicate as husband and wife? How do we make ourselves known, and how do we give others the opportunity to be known? Communication is complicated and tough to understand and navigate. The seven levels of intimacy is a simple model to strengthen the way we communicate in our relationships.

And it's important to get this right. If you ask one hundred people the secret to a successful marriage, most of them will say it is communication. Communication is so important that two entire sessions of BETTER TOGETHER are devoted to it. Let's dig into the seven levels of intimacy model, to provide clarity for how we communicate.

The first level is clichés.

At the first level of communication we speak only in clichés.

Clichés are used to avoid intimacy. We reveal nothing.

The second level is facts.

What do we talk about on this level? The weather. And the football game. And the weather. And what we had for dinner. And the weather.

This level produces something that can pass as a conversation between two people on an elevator, but still, nothing is being revealed. You can have an entire conversation with someone and share absolutely nothing about yourself when dealing at the level of facts.

Can facts lead to intimacy? Sure. But more often than not, like clichés, they are used to avoid it.

The third level of intimacy is opinions.

This third level is the Pandora's box of communication.

This is where the trouble begins because we all have different opinions. Get a crowd together and you won't find two people with the exact same set of beliefs and opinions.

Opinions are formed by two factors: our education and our experiences.

We all have different education and experiences, so we all have different opinions. But when we meet someone who has a different opinion than we do, we act shocked. We act like we have to fight these out. Some married couples fight for years about the same difference of opinion. They can fight so long, they don't even remember what they are fighting about.

The reason for this is simple: We're not good at healthy conflict. And healthy conflict is incredibly important to a marriage. You're going to have conflict in your marriage. And if you don't know how to have healthy conflict, it's going to be really hard to have a thriving marriage. In fact, this is so important that our next session is going to be entirely devoted to dealing with conflict.

The reason so many couples struggle with conflict is because our culture tells us that love is based on understanding. But this sets us up for failure right from the start. The culture says, "I'll love you. . . when I understand you." But what is the most common thing men say? "I don't understand women." The most common thing women say about men? "I don't understand men."

Love is not based on understanding. Love is based on acceptance.

Who are you most likely to reveal yourself to? Someone who judges you? Who is constantly correcting you and putting you down? Of course not. Intimacy is self-revelation, and you are most likely to reveal yourself to someone you feel accepted by.

Intense love does not measure; it just gives.

—St. Teresa of Calcutta

96

The key to intimacy and love is acceptance. We thrive and grow when we feel accepted. Acceptance animates us and helps us strive to be a-better-version-of-ourselves.

And acceptance is a cornerstone of healthy conflict. When we have the maturity to acknowledge that the other person is on a journey to become the-best-version-of-himself or -herself, then we can recognize differences in opinion. We can accept them and help them on their journey. No longer do we need to argue to make ourselves right. We have a higher purpose, an end destination to help them toward.

But when we first encounter the conflict, the temptation is to run from it. When we encounter the level of opinions, the temptation is to surface back to facts or clichés to avoid the conflict. This is the amazing thing about intimacy. We yearn for it, and yet we are afraid of it. It's the one thing we can't live happily without, yet at the first signs of getting there we have to fight the urge to flee.

Can you survive without intimacy? Sure. But you can't be happy without it. And your marriage can't thrive without it.

Pray Together:

ST. ISIDORE OF SEVILLE PRAYER

Holy Spirit,
Be guide of our actions,
indicate the path we should take,
so that with your help,
our work may be in all things pleasing to you.

May you be our only inspiration and the overseer of
our intentions, for you alone possess a glorious name
together with the Father and the Son.

Amen.

Notes

Seven Levels of Intimacy

4.1

4.2

4.3

4.4

4.5

Hopes and Dreams

The fourth level of intimacy is hopes and dreams.

We all have hopes and dreams. And nothing brings us to life like chasing down a dream. Nothing gives us hope and encouragement and excitement like chasing down a dream. And nothing is more satisfying than helping someone else chase down a dream.

Dreams are all around us. You have dreams. I have dreams. Your future husband or wife has dreams. Your friends have dreams. Every stranger you brush up against as you pass through life has dreams too. And one amazing aspect of the human spirit that we often overlook is how natural it is to want to help others chase down their dreams.

One of the first dreams on my dream list was to go surfing. I grew up in Illinois and live in the Midwest, so I don't exactly have ample opportunities to surf. But it was one of the things that just popped into my head in the first fifteen minutes of dreaming, and I wrote it down. Last July my family took a weeklong beach vacation, and I had the joy of spending two hours one morning with my wife and family taking surfing lessons. If I had never written it down, I don't know that I ever would have done it.

When you know someone's dream, you naturally want to help them live that dream. If someone shares a dream with you, you will involuntarily think about that person, their dream, and how you can help them achieve it. It's just a reaction. You don't even have to think about it.

This is why dreams are so essential to relationships. They give us energy and goodwill toward each other. They turn us into advocates for each other. And the benefit isn't just that we get to help someone else achieve their dream. The relationship is two-way.

When you have helped someone achieve their dream, it creates a supernatural bond between you. There is almost nothing that person will not do for you because you helped them achieve their dream.

If you are in a relationship that is struggling, the fourth level of intimacy is your best friend. When you get on this fourth level with someone, it breaks down barriers, heals old wounds, and gives a new direction of hope and excitement to a failing relationship. Two people sharing their dreams changes the way we communicate, interact, and speak to each other. It reveals us in a way that creates vulnerability and powerful goodwill.

Part of the equation is knowing your dreams. In Session 2, you spent time exploring your dreams for your lives. Your dreams will animate your marriage. They will give you hope. They will build your trust and friendship. You will become powerful advocates for each other through the sharing of your dreams.

As husband and wife, one of the best things you can do for your marriage is to get a dream journal together. Get one dream book and share it. Write down your dreams. Share them with each other. Will you talk about it every day? Not likely. But you can't forget about each other's dreams. When we forget about each other's dreams, resentment comes in. That's when we start to think about all the ways we sacrificed for the other person to pursue their dreams while our hopes and dreams were trampled and forgotten.

So make dreams a regular part of your conversation together. Maybe once a month, you take out your dream book and spend fifteen minutes looking at things. You write down your dreams and date them. Then when you go back you can update your progress on some dreams, eliminate some things that aren't really dreams anymore, and experience the joy of crossing off completed dreams.

Dreaming reveals our hopes for the future to each other. It builds excitement and helps us to believe the future will be bigger and better than the past. We become people of possibility when we dream, and that's something every marriage needs.

Exercise:

Get a dream journal together. Write down some of the dreams you shared in Session 2 so you can continue to have regular conversations about your dreams as a couple.

Your dreams
will animate
your marriage.

Feelings

The fifth level of intimacy is feelings.

Feelings. Yes, guys, we're going to talk about our feelings.

Guys get a bad rap for this, don't we? We get a bad rap for our perceived inability to discuss our feelings. This level of intimacy isn't assumed to be our strong suit. Feelings are supposed to be the wife's territory. It's the women's arena; they're the experts.

But the truth is, women aren't always that great with feelings either.

There are five aspects to the fifth level of intimacy:
1. Knowing our feelings
2. Being comfortable expressing our feelings
3. Expressing them at the right time
4. Expressing them in the right place
5. Expressing them to the right person

As a generalization, no, guys aren't always so great at the first two. That's where we get the bad rap when it comes to feelings. But women aren't always so great at the last three. That's how they fall short in their ability to communicate at the fifth level of intimacy.

And this is where the friction comes in. Women excel at the first two aspects; guys struggle with them. Men excel at the last three aspects; women struggle with them. This fundamental difference in our approaches to feelings creates a friction that we've all experienced before.

Part of this friction goes back to that lie told by our culture: that love is based on understanding. See, if love is based on understanding, then every feeling needs to have a reason. Sometimes our feelings are linked to very clear causes:

How was your day?

Great.

Why was it great?

I got a promotion and bought a new car.

How was your day?

Awful.

Why was it awful?

I got fired and wrecked my car.

Cause and effect. Feeling and understanding. Sometimes they go hand in hand.

But other times feelings are much more difficult to express. Sometimes you just really can't get at the reasons for what you are feeling. This is where the lie that love is based on understanding breaks down.

Love isn't based on understanding. Love is based on acceptance. And sometimes we just have to accept that we can't always get at the reasons behind some feelings. And sometimes we have to resist the temptation to "fix" each other's feelings.

When we accept our husband or wife, we don't need to understand their feelings. We can simply be present to them. When our love is based on acceptance, then we are free to be present to celebrate the good, and to come alongside our husband or wife for the bad. Sometimes—many times—that just means being present. In the bad, it's not usually about fixing the problem or understanding the problem; it's almost always about just being present. Men, in particular, often need to be reminded of this; more often than not, your wife just wants you to listen.

Sometimes we are present through our words. Sometimes we are present just by listening and saying nothing at all. Sometimes we are present through helping actions. Sometimes—and this is a key point—we are present by giving the other person space. Being present is about accepting what our spouse is feeling, then giving them what they need in that moment to know they are accepted and loved.

Feelings actually become an area of strength when we remember that love is based on acceptance, not on understanding.

Exercise:

Discuss the five aspects of this level. Where are you strong? Where are you weak? When you are upset, how do you like to be approached? Do you make each other feel accepted or do you constantly strive for understanding? How do you like to be approached when you are experiencing bad feelings? Do you want to be comforted? Do you want to be left alone? Do you want a silent kind gesture? Do you want to be distracted? Write this one thing down and share it with your future spouse.

Come, let's be a comfortable couple, and take care of each other... How glad we shall be that we have somebody we are fond of always, to talk to and sit with.

—Charles Dickens

Seven Levels of Intimacy

Faults, Fears, and Failures

The sixth level of intimacy is fears, faults, and failures.

Fear is a primal driver of the human person, and it will drive you away from the-best-version-of-yourselves if you let it. The most important thing is knowing our fears.

Do you know your fears? Do you know the fears of the people around you? Fears affect us in powerful ways. When we are driven by fear, we do things we would never normally do and say things we would never normally say.

These motivations are fascinating. When we see them, it's an incredible insight into what is going on around us. Sure, what people do and say is interesting, but why they do it and why they say it is fascinating.

For example, when you are at the third level of intimacy and someone shares an opinion, you have to ask: Where did that opinion come from? Why is that your opinion?

You weren't born with opinions. They didn't come preinstalled. So what happened to give you that? What did you do and what was done to you to give you that opinion? What did you learn or see or experience that led you to that opinion?

That's intimacy. The opinion is one thing, but the why—now, that's a whole different thing altogether. Intimacy is getting to the why. Intimacy is self-revelation, and the why is where we reveal ourselves. And nothing kills intimacy like fear.

Consider Adam and Eve. God creates them, they eat the fruit, they realize they're naked, they cover themselves up. Then God shows up and asks Adam where he is. And what is Adam's response? We were naked and afraid, so we hid.

What is our first reaction to fear? To hide. When we are afraid, we don't reveal ourselves, but intimacy is all about self-revelation. When we are afraid, we hide ourselves, and hiding yourself is all about loneliness.

The second aspect of the sixth level is **faults**.

Imagine this: Your husband comes to you and says, "Darling, I've got this fault. I know I have it and I don't want it. I interrupt people all the time and I don't want to. Will you help me overcome it?"

What do you have there? Humility. Vulnerability. Self-revelation.

Then imagine you say, "Yes, I want to help you. But I don't want to call you out in front of other people or nag you, so what is the best way for me to help? Maybe I don't say anything at all; maybe it's just a touch on the arm. Maybe it's a note on your bedside table at the end of the day."

If you have that, you're there. Intimacy. Self-revelation.

But most of the time we spend our lives arguing for our faults, as if they are justified or they are someone else's fault.

The third aspect of the sixth level is **failures**.

We all do stupid things from time to time. A while back a friend of mine was sharing with me what his parents would do when he did something stupid.

His dad would tell him a story about a time in his life when he did a stupid thing. Immediately the floodgates of intimacy were opened as his dad made himself vulnerable and human.

Then his dad would say, "Son, you did a stupid thing. But we can build a path out of here and I want to help you do that. But let's be clear. You did a stupid thing."

When we reveal our humanity we give other people permission to be human. And that is a beautiful thing.

Fear kills intimacy. It makes us run and hide.

Fears, faults, and failures: the sixth level of intimacy. We spend most of our life pretending we don't have any fears, faults, or failures. It should come as no surprise that this level is usually reserved for our most trusted friends and confidants.

And that should tell you how important it is to share them as a married couple. Love each other through the fears, faults, and failures. Share them with each other. Accept them. And you will have an intimacy that every couple dreams of but few really achieve.

Exercise:

Share with your spouse three fears that you have about the future and about yourself. Perhaps take some time to share not only what the fear is, but where that fear comes from. When you are done, exchange your notes and read about each other's fears. Then talk about how you can avoid feeding your future spouse's fears, and how you can help your spouse when you see they are hiding.

Seven Levels of Intimacy

4.1

4.2

4.3

4.4

4.5

Legitimate Needs

The seventh level of intimacy is legitimate needs.

What are legitimate needs? They are needs God gave you that are essential to survival. If you don't have food, you'll die. If you don't have air, you'll die even quicker. These are our legitimate needs.

Why did God give them to us? Because they are clues to what is going to make us happy, plain and simple. If you get really in touch with your legitimate needs, they will reveal to you what will truly make you happy.

We all have the same basic legitimate needs in the four aspects of the human person: **physical, emotional, intellectual, and spiritual**.

Physically we need a good night's sleep, healthy food to nourish our bodies, and exercise. When you have them, you feel great; you feel like a champion. When you don't, you feel awful.

Emotionally we all need to focus on relationships. When your relationships are strong and ordered, you feel better and more fully alive. You are happier.

Intellectually we all need to read great books. Books change our lives. You show me your books and I'll show you what kind of person you are. You show me the books you will read in the next year and I'll show you what kind of person you are going to become. We become the books we read.

Spiritually we need solitude, silence, Scriptures, and sacraments. You're happier when you are immersed in these things, plain and simple.

And the thing about our legitimate needs is they are pretty cheap and simple things. But we ignore them. We set them aside. Why? Because we live in a culture that is consumed with wants.

Happiness is not found in your wants; it is found in your needs. You thrive when your needs are being met.

And this is the pinnacle of intimacy: sharing each other's legitimate needs and helping each other build a life around them. As husband and wife, when you share your legitimate needs and understand your spouse's needs, your marriage will flourish. Your life will be magnified.

The seven levels of intimacy are a model for communication. But they are not a ladder. You won't wake up in the morning and discuss which level you were at yesterday and which level you hope to get to today. No, you'll go in and out of the seven levels all the time. You will go in and out of the seven levels in just one conversation.

What will happen is you will start to notice the seven levels all over the place. Without even thinking about it, you will notice which level you are dealing with. You will recognize it in your conversations and you will now be able to decide not only if you want to go deeper, but how deep you want to go—and you will know how to get there.

What does it take to get there? Carefree timelessness. This is where intimacy takes place. Time together without an agenda, without chores to do, without distractions. Carefree timelessness creates the space to discuss your hopes and dreams, your fears, faults, and failures, and your legitimate needs. This is where acceptance is. This is where intimacy is. This is where love is.

What would happen if you built communication around the deepest levels of intimacy into your marriage? What would happen if you sat down once a month to discuss your dream book? What would happen if you made fears, faults, and failures a part of your regular conversations? What would happen if you sat down every Sunday night to discuss your legitimate needs and how you can support each other in building a life around them?

Ultimately, life is about love, and love takes great communication. And the seven levels of intimacy will help you have a life filled with great conversations.

Exercise:

Set aside a block of time between now and your wedding just for carefree timelessness together. Perhaps it is a full afternoon or two. Maybe it is an entire day or weekend. No agenda, no distractions. Just be together. Use and enjoy that time together as your intimacy builds.

There is no remedy
for love but to love
more.

—Henry David Thoreau

Additional Resources

What the Church, the Bible, and the Saints Teach
Us About the Sacrament of Marriage

Covenant

God initiates a covenant. When the Catholic Church teaches that marriage is a covenant, it is using a rich biblical concept to describe how God's unwavering, exclusive love for his people is a model for the loving union of a married couple. That is the most intimate relationship of all, our permanent covenant.

The Old Testament captures the relationship between God and his chosen people of Israel by speaking of the covenant he offers to them through Abraham and Moses. This covenant is an invitation to enter into a relationship: "I will be your God and you will be my people."

1601 The matrimonial covenant, by which a man and a woman establish between themselves a partnership of the whole of life, is by its nature ordered toward the good of the spouses and the procreation and education of offspring; this covenant between baptized persons has been raised by Christ the Lord to the dignity of a sacrament.

1639 The consent by which the spouses mutually give and receive one another is sealed by God himself. From their covenant arises "an institution, confirmed by the divine law. . . even in the eyes of society." The covenant between the spouses is integrated into God's covenant with man: "Authentic married love is caught up into divine love."

In fact, Jesus says this about the marriage covenant:

But from the beginning of creation, "God made them male and female." "For this reason a man shall leave his father and mother and be joined to his wife, and the two shall become one flesh." So they are no longer two, but one flesh. Therefore what God has joined together, let no one separate.
(Mark 10:6–9)

[We]. . . celebrate the praises of Christ and his Church, the gift of holy love, the sacrament of endless union with God.
—St. Bernard of Clairvaux

Notes

Conflict
Inevitable

Do not forget that true love sets no conditions; it does not calculate or complain, but simply loves.

—St. John Paul II

Conflict Is Inevitable

SESSION 5

Wisdom for Affection from Dr. Vinson

Years ago, I went to the doctor for an examination before having surgery. My regular doctor was unable to see me that day, so I met Dr. Vinson, whom I had never met before. Our conversation at the exam surprised me.

Dr. Vinson told me that she and her husband had recently separated. The two of them had lived together nine years, then they had married and shared that marriage for six more years, having two children in the process. As she reflected with sadness on the demise of their marriage and relationship, she spoke words so poignant that I wrote them down as soon as I left her office:

"Our relationship has been dying a slow, gasping death since the day we married. You don't need love. You need intimacy, trust, concern. A relationship can do without love—it's the others that cannot be replaced."

I disagree with her that a relationship "can do without love." Perhaps she is confusing love with a quickened heartbeat and a breathless moment that really are more for the sizzle period of the relationship.

What deeply strikes me about her words is the desperate, painful pining for attention and affection. "You need intimacy, trust, concern," she said. She's absolutely right about that. Every relationship, every marriage, every person needs those three things.

What she was really saying was, "I yearn to be heard, to be paid attention to, to be loved. I deeply need attention and affection."

We all do. Without those qualities, a relationship will wither and die. Without those, there is no love.

———————————

The two of you are a team.

____

Conflict Is Inevitable

5.1

5.2

5.3

5.4

5.5

Conflict Happens

Do you remember your first fight as a couple? Your first disagreement? I do.

We had moved to Europe for my husband's job, and while he was traveling all over the world and (from my perspective) having a great time, I felt lonely, bored and neglected. When I shared how I was feeling, I expected him to listen well and make me feel better. He responded by asking me if I expected him to quit his job, and told me in no uncertain terms that it wasn't his job to make me happy. The truth is, Leo was under enormous pressure and was afraid of failing in his career. Neither of us was really listening to the other person. Instead of leaning into the conflict, we both shut down. We didn't like how it felt, so we stopped talking and stuffed our feelings. Not a good habit to develop.

Conflict happens.

You'd never know that by watching a Disney movie in which Anna and Kristoff ride off into the future together. Or by watching a romantic comedy, in which the man and woman pursue each other, overcome all kinds of funny obstacles, and land in each other's arms at the end. No one ever mentions that the future might have a few bumps and potholes along the way. It's all happily-ever-after stuff.

So it's easy to think conflict in marriage is bad. That it means we're in trouble and the marriage may not survive it.

That's what Rita thought. She hates conflict. She avoids it any way she can. If the conversation gets a little tense, she will find a way to get distracted by pretending she just got an important text, or she will change the topic altogether. She doesn't like to bring up areas where she and her husband, Joseph, might not see eye-to-eye. She avoids sharing how she feels when her feelings get hurt or she is disappointed.

The goal is not to have zero conflict.

Rita is not willing to invest any energy in honestly sharing her thoughts or opinions when she knows that she and Joseph disagree. She avoids conflict, because she thinks it shows the relationship is in trouble.

Joseph doesn't like conflict. Nobody does. But he doesn't worry about it either. He knows that sometimes people disagree, and he understands that it can take some time to discuss those differences and reach a compromise or resolution. So he doesn't shy away from sharing his feelings when he is struggling or from bringing up an issue that is bothering him in the marriage. He doesn't get angry, but he also doesn't mind feeling a little uncomfortable talking about things, like how he really would prefer that he and Rita not hang out with some of her old friends, who always make him feel left out.

Joseph wants Rita and himself to be better together in every way. He knows that if the relationship is going to grow stronger over time, they will need to discuss areas where they disagree and arrive at a place where they are on the same page. Sometimes that means compromise. Sometimes that just means knowing that they have different opinions and will need to tolerate how the other person feels or sees things. Joseph invests energy to approach Rita with openness and to give what he hopes to receive: caring honesty and a desire to grow stronger as a couple.

Not only is conflict in marriage inevitable; it's perfectly normal. It's a part of life. That's one of the reasons wedding vows include phrases like "for better, for worse," "for richer, for poorer," and "in sickness and in health."

Conflict happens. It occurs in relationships with your family, in relationships at work, in relationships with your friends. And it certainly will occur in your marriage. It happens in all relationships.

Conflict is inevitable. And it can become a source of healthy growth and bonding as a couple. Learning to handle conflict well is an integral part of being married and facing the future together.

**CHURCH VOWS AND
CONSENT**

*I take you for my lawful
wife/husband,
to have and to hold,
from this day forward,
for better, for worse,
for richer, for poorer,
in sickness and in health,
to love and to cherish
until death do us part.*

The goal is not to have zero conflict. Rita's sense that conflict is bad and a sign of weakness is not realistic. Instead, the goal is to find a way to have safe, healthy, constructive conflict. Strong marriages create environments where both spouses feel heard, valued, and loved when conflict occurs. Healthy marriages find ways to resolve conflict and to move forward together. Great marriages provide a safe place for conflict where the result is a better outcome for both spouses.

The two of you are a team. One of the most beautiful aspects of marriage is knowing that you have a teammate who is fully committed to you all the time and who always has your best interest at heart.

Pray Together:

PRAYER OF ST. FRANCIS

**Lord, make me an instrument of your peace.
Where there is hatred, let me sow love;
When there is injury, pardon;
Where there is doubt, faith;
Where there is despair, hope;
Where there is darkness, light;
And where there is sadness, joy.**

**O Divine Master,
Grant that I may not so much seek
To be consoled as to console;
To be understood as to understand;
To be loved as to love;
For it is in giving that we receive;
It is in pardoning that we are pardoned;
And it is in dying that we are born to eternal life.**

Conflict Is Inevitable

5.1

5.2

5.3

5.4

5.5

Common Purpose

I love to travel. I especially love going on our Dynamic Catholic pilgrimages to Rome and Assisi or to the Holy Land. Those places inspire my faith and deepen my love for Catholicism in really special ways. But every time I go, I am always glad to come home. In fact, I usually find someone to hug or high-five once I get through passport control and customs and am back on my home soil in America.

I love America. It's a great country. Traveling reminds me just how good we have things here in the United States. One of the reasons this country has survived and thrived for about 250 years through all kinds of different circumstances is because of our Constitution. That single document reminds us who we are.

We the People of the United States, in Order to form a more perfect Union, establish Justice, insure domestic Tranquility, provide for the common defense, promote the general Welfare, and secure the Blessings of Liberty to ourselves and our Posterity, do ordain and establish this Constitution for the United States of America

It defines our purpose. It lays out how we are going to live together as one people and govern ourselves. And when we disagree, it provides a road map and acts as a reminder for how we will resolve those differences. We have a common purpose to form a more perfect union and secure the blessings of liberty.

Again, as a couple, the two of you are a team. One of the most beautiful aspects of marriage is knowing that you have a teammate who is fully committed to you all the time and who always has your best interests at heart.

In marriage, the two really do become one. It is no longer about the individual ego, but instead about the collective greater good. Everything has to be subordinate to the goal and purpose of the team. Individual achievement means nothing. **Most teams fail not because they lack talent, but because they lack the character necessary to subordinate personal ambition to a common purpose.**

When conflict occurs in the United States, the first thing we do is look at the Constitution and remember our purpose.

What is your purpose as a married couple? You get to establish that for yourselves. Is it to be better together? Or perhaps to help each other become the-best-version-of-yourselves? Maybe it's to help each other get to heaven. You don't have to be ultra-creative and come up with your purpose in haiku or from some long-lost scroll found in the desert. You can choose one of these three options or adapt one of them in a way that suits the two of you.

The point is to know and agree on your common, unchanging purpose as a couple. That way, when you disagree or argue, you can remind yourselves of that purpose. For example, if your purpose is to help each other get to heaven, then the discussion becomes about how your opinions or ideas actually fulfill that shared purpose.

If that is your common purpose, now when you argue, you are arguing for something. You are arguing for the option that actually allows you to help each other get to heaven. You are no longer arguing against something. More important, you are no longer arguing against someone. It is not personal anymore. It is purposeful. And that is a whole different conversation.

Too often, in politics (and even in marriages), arguments are just against something and quickly become personal. Sharing a common purpose frees you to raise the conversation and disagreement to a healthy level. Now it becomes about something constructive. How can we build up our purpose?

And that is what makes conflict healthy and constructive.

Exercise:

Define your common purpose as a married couple. Feel free to use one of the following three options as is or use one as a base to write your own similar purpose.

- To be better together
- To help each other become the-best-version-of-yourselves
- To help each other get to heaven

People are weird. When we find someone with weirdness that is compatible with ours, we team up and call it love.

—Dr. Seuss

Conflict Is Inevitable

5.1

5.2

5.3

5.4

5.5

Three Kinds of Couples

We all know a couple like Sam and Betsy. They argue a lot. In fact, they even seem to enjoy it. When they argue, Sam and Betsy each get very intense and emotional. They usually dig in their heels and cling to their positions no matter what. At times, Betsy expresses anger, but she never insults or demeans her husband. Sam often shares his insecurities, but he is careful not to criticize or disrespect his wife. Neither of them bullies the other. Oddly, Sam and Betsy find ways to inject humor and laughter into their debates and arguments, and they seem to come out of the arguments more connected than ever.

Relationship experts (like Harold Raush and John and Julie Gottman) like to label Sam and Betsy's style of managing conflict as "volatile." When both partners embody the volatile style of resolving conflict, the marriage tends to grow and be satisfying.

Lucas and Michelle, on the other hand, would swim across the ocean to avoid arguing. They feel uncomfortable sharing what they need from each other and often see themselves as two different people with different sets of interests. In fact, they avoid conflict so much that they would say they have no arguments or disagreements in their marriage. Although they do tend to agree about a lot, they really just do not want to invest any energy in working through the areas where they do not agree. In some areas, the two of them feel very connected; the other areas, they choose to ignore. For personalities like Lucas and Michelle, the relationship works. Their style is very different from Sam and Betsy's, but it works for them.

Just as relationship experts would label Sam and Betsy as "volatile," they would classify Lucas and Michelle as "avoiders." Again, when the wife and husband share the style of avoiding conflict, the marriage tends to work for them.

Allen and Lucy represent a third kind of couple. It is important to Allen to listen and understand what Lucy is thinking and how she feels. Lucy likes for Allen to express his thoughts, and she listens intently when he does. Neither of them is overly emotional, and they are careful to show affection and concern for each other regularly. There are certainly issues that the two of them do not discuss, and sometimes their arguments can become difficult. Yet Allen and Lucy usually find a way to turn down the heat in the conversation and look for an opportunity to reach a compromise.

Experts would usually call Allen and Lucy "understanders." They don't avoid conflict, but neither do they enjoy it or seek it out. They recognize that conflict is inevitable, and on most subjects, they are able to find a path forward together. When both husband and wife are understanders, they tend to be happy and satisfied with their marriage.

You've probably noticed with these three couples that both the wife and the husband share the same approach to conflict resolution. And you've probably noticed that that common ground usually leads to a satisfying marriage, even though some people would look at one of these styles and say, "I could never be married to someone who acts like that!"

Challenges arise, however, when the man and the woman have different approaches to conflict. For example, if Sam and his volatile style were married to Michelle, who avoids conflict, the two of them would struggle ever to find common ground. In the same way, if Lucy and her understanding style were married to Lucas, who avoids conflict at all costs, the two of them would be likely to grow increasingly frustrated over time.

Sharing the same conflict style will certainly make communication easier for you over time. But whether you do or not, there are conflict and communication principles that will be richly valuable to you in building a foundation for your marriage and family. **Remember purpose. Breathe deeply. Listen attentively. Accept responsibility. Speak respectfully.**

These principles are crucial tools to help you become better together. They'll be the focus of the next session.

Exercise:

Take a look at yourself. What kind of conflict style do you tend to have? Now think of your groom- or bride-to-be. What kind of conflict style does he or she bring to the relationship?

What Nobody Tells You as a Woman

Written by Anita, a Dynamic Catholic Ambassador

The culture lied to me. I was always told, "You can do everything," "There's no sacrifice in having kids." "You can have it all and do it all," they told me time and again.

But then I had my first child, a daughter, and everything changed. I changed. As soon as she was born, I knew I was intimately and physically connected to her in a profound way that was different from my husband's connection with her. It just happened. Being a mother does that. It changes you. It ushers in a beautiful new chapter of life that no one can fully prepare you for. You. A mother.

My husband loved me, and he loved our little girl. He changed diapers and helped with baby duties. But I quickly realized this was not fifty-fifty anymore. Nobody else could be her mother. My husband had an important role to play but he was not her mother. It was a metamorphosis that is difficult to describe, but I knew the moment I held her that her needs came first. Life shifted.

I began to worry I might lose all my professional dreams. No one had prepared me for this. I had always bought the culture's lie that you can do everything, and you are defined by your job. But that just wasn't true. Only in time did I begin to consider the idea that you can do everything, just not all at once. I came to realize you have to sacrifice, no matter what. That's just how it is.

Here is what I wish someone had told me going into marriage:

1. Having a family requires sacrifice; there's no way around it. But your family is going to be the best thing that ever happens to you. Period. Sacrifice doesn't look the same for everyone. For some women it means staying home to support their family. For others it means working to support their family. Either way, it's a sacrifice. We live out priorities and sacrifice for our families in different ways, and that's OK. Don't worry how everyone else does it. Families require sacrifice because love requires sacrifice.
2. Yes, you can do everything, just not all at once. We treat the decisions around career and family like they are so final and absolute, but the truth is that life comes in chapters. And chapters change.

Keys to Healthy Conflict

Most people think relationships are about giving and taking. But in healthy relationships, there is no taking, only giving and receiving.

Relationships are about teamwork, not about getting what you want. In fact, relationships are not about getting at all. They are about giving and receiving, about working together for the common good.

One of the obstacles we encounter in teamwork is ego. The ultimate dysfunction in a relationship occurs when the individuals seek personal fulfillment at the expense of the team.

You and your spouse are a team. You share a common, unchanging purpose. How's your team doing?

Everything has to become subordinate to the goal and purpose of the team. If the team loses, everyone loses. Intimacy and marriage require teamwork. When conflict arises, husband and wife must have a plan for how to navigate through the conflict for the good of the team.

That plan will always include:

1.   Remember purpose.

You have agreed on your common, unchanging purpose as a couple. When you disagree, remind yourselves of that purpose. Frame the conversation around how this disagreement can help you fulfill your purpose as a couple. For example, if your purpose is to help each other become the-best-version-of-yourselves, then the focus of the discussion becomes how your opinions or ideas actually can make that happen.

Now you are arguing for something; you are no longer arguing against something. Most important, you are no longer arguing against someone. It is no longer personal. It is purposeful.

2. **Breathe deeply.**

Thomas Jefferson famously said, "When angry count to ten before you speak. If very angry, count to one hundred." He was right. Taking a break when conflict arises can be your good friend. Do something that relaxes you. Slow down. Take a walk. Listen to soothing music. Inhale deeply. All of these can calm the process and help you focus on teamwork rather than on being an individual.

Slowing the process can help you focus on your partner and what they are feeling and also help you delay the need to express your own thoughts and feelings. It creates space in the conversation and prevents you from taking things personally or losing your cool.

3. **Listen attentively.**

We all desire to be heard. It is one of the ways we feel most loved. This is especially true with our husband or wife. This person who matters most to us can give us the greatest gift of love by simply listening to our deepest feelings and hurts, maintaining eye contact so we know they are seeking to know us deeply, and occasionally offering a word of kindness even when they may disagree with part of what we say.

By simply listening attentively to your spouse, you are de-escalating the situation and offering love right in the middle of an argument. You are communicating acceptance even in disagreement.

4. **Accept responsibility.**

Healthy people accept at least partial responsibility for the issue. They do not retreat into defensiveness and refuse to accept any blame whatsoever. Healthy people own their actions and words. They do not resort to excuse making.

The act of accepting responsibility underscores the fact that you two are a team. And it points toward a way forward in which both of you create the solution, rather than basing your view on I win/you lose. When both spouses accept responsibility, the relationship moves toward a "we win" model of teamwork.

5. **Speak respectfully.**

Teamwork requires respect. And respect leaves no room for name-calling, stonewalling, sarcastic ridiculing, or manipulation.

Instead, respect will move openly toward someone with positive energy. Respect will remember that sometimes it is more important to be loving than to be right. And respect will give what we expect to receive in return.

In the end, the goal of managing conflict is not to be right. The goal is to grow stronger by listening, loving, and finding a healthy way forward. Compromise is good. In fact, it's better than good; it's wonderful.

But sacrifice can be even greater than compromise. Sacrifice sets faithful Catholic marriages apart from the culture. Selfless love sacrifices for the good of the other. And when both spouses embrace the selfless, sacrificial love embodied in Jesus, the marriage gains a supernatural, divine strength.

You and your spouse are a team.

Discuss:

What might the following passage of Scripture teach you about handling conflict in your marriage?

Be angry but do not sin; do not let the sun go down on your anger, and do not make room for the devil. . . Let no evil talk come out of your mouths, but only what is useful for building up, as there is need, so that your words may give grace to those who hear. . . Put away from you all bitterness and wrath and anger and wrangling and slander, together with all malice, and be kind to one another, tenderhearted, forgiving one another, as God in Christ has forgiven you. (Ephesians 4:26–32)

....
....
....
....
....
....
....
....
....
....
....
....
....
....
....
....
....
....
....
....
....

Teamwork requires respect.

5.1

5.2

Conflict Is Inevitable

5.3

5.4

5.5

Laugh!

If someone were watching you have a conflict as a couple, what would they be thinking? Imagine you accidentally butt-dialed your mother while you and your partner were fighting and she could hear the whole thing. Would she see it as serious, humorous, dangerous, entertaining, or as something else? What does your answer say about your relationship, and what might God want to teach you from that?

The most undervalued ingredient in healthy relationships is a sense of humor. The ability to laugh at yourself. The ability to laugh with your spouse. The joy of laughing together at life. The liberty of accepting each other in spite of your shortcomings.

Have you ever spent time with a humorless person? There is no worse thing in life than that! The closest distance between two people is humor. Humor can actually build intimacy.

In fact, lacking humor often leads to conflict in the first place. That's because humor is often the release valve that can take some of the steam out of a disagreement. It's a central and natural part of strong marriages and strong relationships. Yet it is often neglected or dismissed.

Laughter relieves stress. It creates a lightheartedness and helps us enjoy life at a higher level. Humor lifts the human spirit.

At the same time, we have to be careful of negative humor, in which we make fun of or even demean the other person. That negative humor can be especially damaging when used in front of other people. Resist the cheap laugh. It's the average comedian who tells a bunch of dirty or degrading jokes and makes everyone feel awkward and uncomfortable so that they will laugh. A great comedian doesn't need dirty or cheap, demeaning jokes. Life is funny enough.

So it just may be that the best thing you can add to your conflict style as a couple is to ask, "What's the funniest thing that happened today?" or "What's the funniest thing you heard about today?"

Answering those questions quickly reframes your feelings and conversations and injects a lightness into the room.

It just may be that when you feel like fighting, the most productive next step is to watch a comedian or a funny movie for thirty minutes before you begin discussing whatever you are disagreeing about. Doing that together changes the argument. George Bernard Shaw understood this very well. "If you want to tell people the truth," he remarked, "make them laugh; otherwise they will kill you."

Finally, remember that conflict is inevitable, but it can be healthy and productive, and great marriages learn from their conflicts how to be better together. People in great marriages also know that more often than not, you will look back on your disagreements or arguments with a deeper perspective, and you will realize just how petty or self-centered you were. Better yet, you will often see just how humorous that argument or dispute really was. Truly, your conflicts will often later become sources of great humor for you both. That is a sign of a great marriage.

Humor will be your best friend.

Exercise:

Ask your beloved, "What is the funniest thing that happened today?" Or "What is the funniest thing you heard about today?" Laugh together.

....

....

....

....

....

....

....

....

....

....

....

....

....

....

....

....

....

....

....

....

....

....

....

....

....

....

....

One word frees us

of all the weight

and pain of life:

That word is love.

—Sophocles

144

Additional Resources

What the Church, the Bible, and the Saints Teach
Us About the Sacrament of Marriage

The Model of Christ and His Bride, the Church: Sacrificial Love

As a sacrament, marriage is rooted in the sacrificial love that Jesus has for the Church. In fact, the Scriptures describe the Church as the bride of Christ. Just as Christ loved the Church and gave himself up for her in love, so too does that sacrificial love become the model for man and wife. After all, love is most deeply expressed in sacrifice.

That means a husband's mission is to love his wife as Christ loves the Church and gave himself up for her. A husband is to lay down his life for his bride to help her get to heaven. What a beautiful image for marriage.

CATECHISM

1661 The sacrament of Matrimony signifies the union of Christ and the Church. It gives spouses the grace to love each other with the love with which Christ has loved his Church; the grace of the sacrament thus perfects the human love of the spouses, strengthens their indissoluble unity, and sanctifies them on the way to eternal life.

SCRIPTURE

Be subject to one another out of reverence for Christ.

Wives, be subject to your husbands as you are to the Lord. For the husband is the head of the wife just as Christ is the head of the church, the body of which he is the Savior. Just as the church is subject to Christ, so also wives ought to be, in everything, to their husbands.

Husbands, love your wives, just as Christ loved the church and gave himself up for her, in order to make her holy by cleansing her with the washing of water by the word, so as to present the church to himself in splendor, without a spot or wrinkle or anything of the kind—yes, so that she may be holy and without blemish. In the same way, husbands should love their wives as they do their own bodies. He who loves his wife loves himself. For no one ever hates his own body, but he nourishes and tenderly cares for it, just as Christ does for the church, because we are members of his body. "For this reason a man will leave his father and mother and be joined to his wife, and the two will become one flesh." This is a great mystery, and I am applying it to Christ and the church. Each of you, however, should love his wife as himself, and a wife should respect her husband.
(Ephesians 5:21–33)

SAINT

We can do no great things; only small things with great love.
—St. Teresa of Calcutta

Notes

The love of husband and wife is the

force that welds society together.

—St. John Chrysostom

Prayer and Spirituality

SESSION 6

Wisdom for Legacy from Harry and Regina

———————

Harry and Regina's story made the news across America. These two enjoyed a lifelong romantic relationship. And they worked at it. They went to Mass together, prayed together, played cards together, and shared nearly every aspect of life. Attention and affection saturated their relationship. They had little habits, like on Saturday nights, when they watched television, they'd sit on the couch together and hold hands. When music came on, their children would help their mom stand up so she could sway because she loved to dance. Harry used to say that Regina could make any man look like a good dancer because she was so good.

Harry and Regina welcomed six children into the world, followed by fourteen grandchildren. Harry saw himself as Regina's protector over the course of their sixty-five years of marriage. He worked as a teacher, principal, and coach in the local school system; she worked as a school secretary after being a stay-at-home mom. They lived in the same home for decades, until they needed greater care and moved to another town to be near their daughter, a nurse.

In the nursing home, the caregiver would tuck Regina in each night. Then Harry would go in and bless her with holy water and give her a kiss. That was part of their nightly ritual.

Their daughter, Karen, said, "When Mom became ill, we tried to make it clear to Dad that Mom wasn't going to make it, and he seemed really agitated for a day or so, at first.

And then he became really calm, and I think he decided, 'No she's not going without me.'

Mom had said that she didn't want to be here without Dad. They were just so devoted to one another."

Harry died on a Sunday morning at 7:30, at the age of 91. Regina died later that evening, at 6:30, at the age of 89. They both passed away in the room they'd shared for the past two months in a nursing home.

Harry and Regina would have celebrated their sixty-sixth wedding anniversary just a week later. Instead, they fulfilled their wish of crossing the river and going home together. "I think we all agreed it was no coincidence," said their daughter.

Best of all, their family decided to celebrate Harry and Regina's sixty-five-year union with a joint funeral Mass in their home parish. The granddaughters carried Regina's casket; the grandsons carried Harry's.

Now, that is a legacy of faith and love.

———————

Dig the well before you get thirsty.

———

6.1

6.2

6.3

6.4

6.5

What Best Friends Do

Marriage is hard work.

The fairy tale romance is just that: a fairy tale. Life is filled with ups and downs, joys, struggles, successes, challenges, sickness, financial difficulties, celebrations, hurt feelings, and expectations gaps. Marriage doesn't take all that away. It doesn't give you a way around life, but it does give you someone to go through life with.

Couples with dynamic marriages know there will be difficulties. And because they expect it, they aren't afraid when those difficulties arrive. They also know that the hard work of marriage is the best kind of hard work because you get to do it with your best friend. The hard work of marriage only feels wrong to the person who believes marriage shouldn't be hard work.

Couples with dynamic marriages also know they will need a lot of resources for their marriage to thrive. They will look for and utilize resources like those offered through Dynamic Catholic. They will listen to talks or read books about thriving marriages. They will attend marriage events offered in their area. And they will be constantly on the lookout for other couples who appear to have dynamic marriages, so they can ask their advice.

Of all the resources God has given us for marriage, two are game changers.

The first is prayer. When things get difficult, we naturally turn to prayer. But couples with dynamic marriages build prayer into their marriage before things get difficult, so they already have the habit established when they need it. They know the old wisdom: Dig the well before you are thirsty. These couples turn to God, and they ask for his leadership and guidance. They ask God to coach them in their marriage. There are many forms of prayer—times when we praise God, worship God, and confess to God. But establishing a habit of prayer in which we turn to God for guidance is critical to a dynamic marriage.

God loves each of us as if there were only one of us.

—St. Augustine

When it comes to building prayer into your relationship, start with something simple, and start now. What might happen if you set the alarm on your phone for noon every day, and when that alarm went off you each prayed a quick Our Father for the intention of your upcoming wedding? This daily habit will connect you more as a couple, and the little interruption will train you to focus your day around God and each other. Your wedding will be surrounded with this intention and reap benefits you won't even be able to see.

The second game-changing resource is finding a mentor couple. What a gift to gain encouragement and wisdom from another couple who is further along in their state in life and who embodies the dynamic marriage you are dreaming of.

If you wanted to be the best in the world at something, what would you do? If you thought about it seriously, one of the things you would absolutely do is find someone who can coach you. Mentor couples serve as that kind of coach. They will help you approach your marriage with the goal of making it the best ever.

Marriages need coaching, advice, and encouragement from time to time. God has given us so many resources for marriage, but many couples wait too long to tap into those resources. Find a mentor couple. Pray together. Tap into life-giving resources for your marriage now, so you have a well of strength to pull from when things get tough. Dig the well before you get thirsty.

Exercise:
Take a first step now: Set your phone alarm for noon tomorrow and say a brief prayer or Our Father for the intention of your wedding and marriage.

Notes

Prayer and Spirituality

World-Class Help

When you look around, you probably see a lot of married couples with problems that you hope to avoid in your marriage. You might have even thought that, knowing your relationship and the person you are going to marry, you could never get to the place where you would be dealing with the kinds of problems some people are dealing with.

Understand this: Those couples you are looking at felt exactly how you feel now. There is a good chance they don't want and never wanted a marriage like that either.

Marriage is difficult, and problems do arise.

Couples with dynamic marriages are aware that they will need help along the way, and it comes in many forms. One of the deepest wells for help in a marriage is spiritual help. And one of the greatest forms of spiritual help comes from a habit of prayer. Prayer builds self-awareness, which is essential to any healthy and dynamic relationship.

For decades, the time we spend in focused prayer has been diminishing as our lives have become busier and busier. We rush from one urgent thing to the next. The problem with this is that the most important things are hardly ever urgent. Prayer is one of those important things. Prayer helps us identify what matters most and strengthens our hearts and minds to give priority to those things in our daily lives. What could be more important than prayer?

Without prayer, over time we forget the qualities that make us uniquely human (compassion, generosity, humility, fortitude), and we become more and more like mere animals.

Prayer leads us to catch a glimpse of the-best-version-of-ourselves. It helps us develop the virtue necessary to celebrate our best selves. In marriage, prayer fortifies our love for our spouse; it encourages us to collaborate with God for a dynamic and healthy relationship. Most crucial of all, prayer sustains us when marriage gets difficult.

Look at a healthy marriage and you will find men and women of prayer. Is it enough for them just to pray? No. Life is complex and difficult, and at times we will need to turn to resources like books, mentor couples, marriage events, and marriage counselors. But the best action springs forth from a vibrant prayer life.

The best place to start is an honest assessment of where you are. In this book, you will find a helpful exercise to complete as a couple. This is going to help you and your future spouse get a real sense of where you are in your spiritual journeys.

Once you know where you are, you can take a look at three areas of your life to help you know where to go.

First, where can you shore up your own spiritual life? As you conducted your honest self-assessment, you probably noticed an area or two of potential growth. That is only a good thing. Ask God to show you the best next steps in grasping those opportunities to grow spiritually.

Second, decide your spirituality as a couple. What is your prayer life going to look like? When life happens and things start to slip, how will you give each other permission to hold the other accountable? Don't be vague here. Get specific. When, where, and how will you pray? How will you incorporate reading Scripture or other spiritual books? Leave no stone unturned when it comes to planning your spiritual lives together.

Third, decide how you will engage and pray with your community. Do you belong to a parish? When and where do you go to Mass? How are you getting to know the people in your parish? How are you supporting them and letting them support you? When you are married, how will you serve the community?

These three areas of your spiritual life will build the spiritual bedrock of your marriage. The rest of this session digs into each of these areas further, because when the foundation is strong, the house stands, plain and simple. With these three aspects of your spiritual life established at the start of your marriage, you will be ready to weather the storms that come with life.

Exercise:

1. Write down your spiritual history in one page. Include:
    - How did your family practice the faith?
    - What do you remember as an important tradition in your family's faith life?
    - When did the faith become important to you? Why?
    - If it is not important to you, why is that?
    - What are your spiritual habits?
    - Describe your prayer life.
    - When was the last time you read a good Catholic book?
    - Describe your giving habits.

2. As you seek to move toward the-best-version-of-yourself individually and as a couple, start with a short self-evaluation. How would you rank yourself in each of these areas? Circle the number that corresponds to how much you see this area prospering in your life, with a score of 1 being very little and 10 being the fullest abundance you could ever imagine. Doing this will help you envision where and how you will grow as you seek to become the-best-version-of-yourself.

LOVE

1   2   3   4   5   6   7   8   9   10

JOY

1   2   3   4   5   6   7   8   9   10

PEACE

1   2   3   4   5   6   7   8   9   10

PATIENCE

1   2   3   4   5   6   7   8   9   10

KINDNESS

1   2   3   4   5   6   7   8   9   10

GENEROSITY

1   2   3   4   5   6   7   8   9   10

FAITHFULNESS

1   2   3   4   5   6   7   8   9   10

GENTLENESS

1   2   3   4   5   6   7   8   9   10

SELF-CONTROL

1   2   3   4   5   6   7   8   9   10

Tobiah rose from bed and said to his wife, "My sister, come, let us pray and beg our Lord to grant us mercy and protection."

She got up, and they started to pray and beg that they might be protected. He began with these words:

"Blessed are you, O God of our ancestors;
blessed be your name forever and ever!
Let the heavens and all your creation bless you forever.

You made Adam, and you made his wife Eve
to be his helper and support;
and from these two the human race has come.
You said, 'It is not good for the man to be alone;
let us make him a helper like himself.'

Now, not with lust,
but with fidelity I take this kinswoman as my wife.
Send down your mercy on me and on her,
and grant that we may grow old together.
Bless us with children."

They said together, "Amen, amen!"
Then they went to bed for the night.

(Tobit 8:4–9)

Prayer and Spirituality

—————

Our Lives Change When Our Habits Change

Our lives change when our habits change.

If you want to get healthier, change your exercise and eating habits. If you want to have healthier relationships, change the way you spend time with and talk to people. And if you want to get spiritually healthy, change your spiritual habits.

The number one habit you can build for a healthier spiritual life is prayer.

A few months ago I was visiting a grade school, and a child, perhaps seven years old, asked me, "Why do you pray?" Sometimes a question is so simple that it causes you to pause to ponder the answer.

I know all the right answers to that question. The *Catechism* tells us that the purposes and forms of prayer are adoration, petition, intercession, thanksgiving, and praise. But I knew this answer would not satisfy my curious young friend.

So I asked him the same question he had asked me: "Why do you pray?"

He didn't have to think about it. Spontaneously he said, "Well, God is my friend, and friends like to know what is going on in each other's lives."

Prayer is the single most important habit for a healthy spiritual life. For highly engaged Catholics, God is not some distant force, but rather a personal friend and adviser. They are trying to listen to the voice of God in their lives. They believe doing God's will is the only path that leads to lasting happiness.

Are we saying the rest of Catholics don't pray? No. But their prayer tends to be spontaneous and inconsistent. Highly engaged Catholics, in contrast, have a daily commitment to prayer, a routine. Prayer is a priority for them. They also have a structured way of praying. Many of them pray at the same time every day. The routine they follow during that prayer time varies from person to person, but they tend to abide by their own individual structure. It's a habit.

Many of us are taught one kind of prayer, and we lock into that for all our lives. But life changes and brings new seasons. What was once challenging and exciting becomes dull and routine. What was once empty and hollow can later have meaning and purpose.

Consider silence. When two people are first dating, silence can be excruciating. On a first date, it can be the kiss of death for a future relationship. But over time as a relationship develops into a great love, two people often learn to enjoy just being with each other in silence. Once their relationship reaches this stage, far from being awkward, the silence can be comforting and powerful. They have learned just to be with each other.

A great life of prayer develops in the same way. At first the silence can be excruciating, almost torturous. But over time we learn to tolerate it, and then to enjoy it. Before long we find ourselves yearning for more and more of it.

Clarity emerges from silence. You know this instinctively. If you are taking a road trip with a car full of people and you get lost, what does the driver ask everyone to do? Turn off the music and be quiet. Why? When you need laser clarity, you want silence. And people who live with high levels of passion and purpose are not afraid of spending some time alone in silence with God.

Quiet is critical to our spiritual development because it is in the silence that God speaks to us. We pray for many reasons, and one of those reasons is to seek the will of God for our lives. Without silence it becomes almost impossible to discern God's will.

God desires nothing but good things for us. So when we speak of following the will of God, we are entering into a process of discernment to discover the good that he desires for us. "God, what do you

BEST ADVENT EVER, a Dynamic
Catholic Email Program
December 2017

*As a volunteer teacher of our
faith, I am constantly telling
young people about spending
time in silence. My small group
is usually twelve to fifteen ninth-
grade boys. When speaking
about silence, I compare it to
the two-minute drill in football. Spend two minutes to get
quiet—no device, no music,
just silence. Just two minutes.
If those guys can spend hours
concentrating on two minutes
and it changes the game, why
can't we spend time to change
ourselves?*

*That's how I started years ago.
Now every morning I try to
spend ten minutes in silence. It is
when I don't do this that my day
is more hectic than I wish. Spend
some time in silence. Just two
minutes—it will change your day.
I promise.*

—David

think I should do?" I call this the big question. It has been my experience that it is the only question that leads to peace and fulfillment.

In the silence the voice of God will speak to you. He will give you
awareness of what is happening in various aspects of your life. He
will help you see what matters most and what matters least. He will
help you see how your life together and your marriage continue to
grow and develop. He will announce changes in the seasons of life
and help you adapt to those changes.

Finally, I want to help facilitate the growth of silence and prayer in
your spiritual life. The Dynamic Catholic Prayer Process was developed with some of the Church's most ancient wisdom regarding
prayer. The result is a process that is fully adaptable to your state
in life and your experience with prayer. The process goes like this:

The Prayer Process

1. Gratitude: Begin by thanking God in a personal dialogue for
   whatever you are most grateful for today.

2. Awareness: Revisit the times in the past twenty-four hours
   when you were and were not the-best-version-of-yourself.
   Talk to God about these situations and what you learned
   from them.

3. Significant Moments: Identify something you experienced
   today and explore what God might be trying to say to you
   through that event (or person).

4. Peace: Ask God to forgive you for any wrong you have committed (against yourself, another person, or him) and to fill you
   with a deep and abiding peace.

5. Freedom: Speak with God about how he is inviting you to
   change your life so that you can experience the freedom to be
   the-best-version-of-yourself.

6. **Others**: Lift up to God anyone you feel called to pray for today, asking him to bless and guide them.

7. Finish by praying the **Our Father**.

Each of the first six steps in the process should stimulate a conversation with God. It is easy to fall into the trap of merely thinking about these things. When you find yourself doing that, return to actually speaking with God about whatever it is you are thinking. The goal is to develop the ability to have intimate conversations with God during this time set aside for prayer. The more deeply rooted we become in this daily habit of prayer, the more those conversations with God will spill over into the moments of our daily lives.

If you are just beginning, you may want to start with just one minute of conversation with God each day, adding a minute each week until you reach ten. If you decide to do this, don't try to race through all seven aspects of the prayer process. Just use the first step, Gratitude. Spend your minute speaking to God about everyone and everything you are grateful for, and then close with an Our Father. As you extend your time spent in prayer over the coming weeks, I suggest you add one step at a time of the process to your daily prayer. The key is to get the conversation started.

But whether you start with one minute a day or ten minutes a day, I hope this session has left you thinking, "I can do that!" Nothing will change your life more meaningfully than developing a vibrant and sustainable prayer life.

Exercise:
Let's take a few moments and pray through this process together, right now—this very moment.

In the name of the Father . . .

Notes

Prayer and Spirituality

6.1

6.2

6.3

6.4

6.5

How Will You Pray?

As your prayer life goes, so goes your spiritual life. And without a strong spiritual life, it will be harder to weather the difficulties you will face in life and in marriage. By now you have come to realize that prayer is going to form the bedrock of your spiritual life as a couple.

So the question becomes: How will you pray as a couple? How will you keep the spiritual bedrock of your marriage strong?

The first thing to know is that this is not a question you answer once and are done with. This question should be a regular part of your conversation as a married couple. Your marriage will enter different seasons of life, with different requirements for each new season. Here are just a few of the ages and stages your marriage will go through:

- *The sizzle of dating and the thrill of courtship and engagement.*
- *The settling down of beginning a new life together as a married couple.*
- *The transition to parenthood as children arrive.*
- *The rediscovery of each other as mates when the nest empties and you are alone together again.*
- *The celebration and welcoming of grandchildren and great-grandchildren.*
- *The caregiving as health issues and aging begin to exact their toll.*

During the changing stages of life and marriage, your prayer life will need to change too. As a child, you might only learn to pray the Our Father. As you grow, you might add in a simple prayer before meals and a prayer before bed. As an adult you might begin to stop by church and pray, listening to the Holy Spirit.

You very recently entered into a new season of life. Engagement is a season of life entirely different from dating. Soon you will be married and enter another new season of life. With these changing seasons will come changes and growth to your prayer life too.

One of the important things to keep in mind is to continually ask yourself what your prayer life could look like as a couple. Let's take a look at three examples of how to pray as a couple.

THE PRAYER PROCESS

In the previous section we talked about using the Prayer Process. This beautiful process of prayer isn't just for your personal prayer life. It can be done with your spouse, and when it is, it takes on a whole new dimension.

Slowly build this simple little habit into your daily life as a couple, and open yourself to a wellspring of God's presence. Best of all, watch that wellspring of your prayer life bear fruit in the lives of your family and children.

NEXT SUNDAY'S GOSPEL

Another great way to pray with your husband or wife is by reading with them. Reading nurtures the mind and settles the soul. It lets you see things you've never seen, experience things you've never experienced, and get a glimpse of the best life has to offer.

Read Scripture. Pick a night each week that you will spend together to read the Gospel for Sunday and talk about what stands out to you. Slowly build this habit into your marriage. You will be amazed how your knowledge and enthusiasm for the faith will begin to grow. You will also get to know Jesus in the Gospels. And when you go to Mass, you will be prepared in an entirely new way.

THE ROSARY

The Rosary works. It will fill you with an incredible sense of peace.

There is just something about it that settles our hearts and minds. It puts things in perspective and allows us to see them as they really are. If you allow it, the Rosary will change your life.

To experience the tremendous fruits of the Rosary, establish it as a spiritual habit in your life and marriage.

Go to **dynamiccatholic.com** to get your copy of the book *Rediscover the Rosary* to help you establish this habit.

When you develop a prayer habit in your marriage, you will thrive in a way you could never have anticipated. New strengths will emerge. God will begin to open vistas on your future and your family. A regular prayer habit isn't just a good thing to do for your marriage; it's pouring the foundation for your life.

Exercise:

Pick one of these three forms of prayer and begin to develop the habit as a couple. Don't pick all three—don't try to do everything and end up doing nothing.

Pick one of these three life-giving forms of prayer and resolve to establish it as a habit in your life. Maybe it's praying the Rosary once a month. Maybe it's reading the Gospel for Mass together each week. Maybe it's finding a time and place every day to pray the Prayer Process together.

If you miss a day, just press on. If you forget, don't worry about it. If you feel like it isn't working, just keep going. Trust that God will meet you in your prayers together. That's the secret to establishing a habit.

Prayer and Spirituality

6.1

6.2

6.3

6.4

6.5

What Will Your Contribution Be?

Everyone wants to belong to a dynamic parish.

It's amazing, isn't it? Even people who never go to Mass still want to belong to a dynamic parish. Of course, if you stop and ask most people what it means for a parish to be dynamic, they don't really have many specific ideas. It's as if they aren't sure what a dynamic parish looks like, but they'll know it when they see it.

On the other hand, complaints about parishes aren't difficult to find.

The music is lifeless. The homilies are boring. The people are mean. There isn't enough parking. The doughnuts after Mass are stale. There isn't enough programming for old people. There isn't enough programming for young people. There are too many programs. You get the picture.

But there is a question that isn't being asked nearly enough.

What are you doing to make your parish thrive?

I mean, it's a natural question, right? You're getting married in the Catholic Church, you're going to belong to a parish, and you're going to want to belong to a dynamic parish—so what will your contribution be?

Maybe you've never thought about your contribution before. That's OK. How do you contribute to your parish? Are you helping it thrive? Consider this for a moment: If every member of your parish contributed at the same level as you are, what would the parish be like?

One of the main ways you contribute to your parish is through your presence at Mass. But what do you bring to the Mass? Do you bring your attention, your enthusiasm, and your expectation? Do you anticipate God's voice and respond with your whole heart? Or do you go out of obligation, simply going through the motions?

If you feel like your contribution at Mass could be a little better, remember: Our lives change when our habits change.

Consider your habits around the Mass. What rituals do you have when it comes to attending Mass?

Do you always go at the same time? How do you dress? What time do you arrive? Where do you sit? Do you respond out loud, just move your lips, respond in your mind, or zone out? What do you do before Mass? What do you do after?

Now is a great time to sit down with your future spouse and consider your rituals surrounding the Mass.

A few years back my wife and I decided we needed to improve our rituals surrounding the Mass. We were having more kids and they were getting older, so attending Mass was just plain getting difficult for our family. So we decided to change a few things.

First, we began reading the Gospel readings in the car on the way to Mass. My wife would read, and the kids would quietly listen in the back. This would help them get focused for what was to come.

Second, we began sitting in the first few pews of the church. This isn't for everyone, but for us it made a huge difference. The kids could actually see what was going on and therefore paid more attention.

Third, we began getting doughnuts after church. We wanted to create a sense of excitement around Sunday morning and the Mass. Now the kids know that every Sunday we are going to go to Mass and get doughnuts as a special treat for the family. We don't use this as a reward for good behavior or a punishment for bad behavior. It's just part of the routine.

Fourth, we ask the kids every Sunday morning at the doughnut shop what God said to them during the Mass. Over time, they began to expect God to say something to them at Mass. They listened and paid attention. After Mass, at the doughnut shop, they wanted to share what they had heard that week. And we write it down in our Mass Journals each week so we can look back at it later.

These four rituals surrounding our Sunday Mass experience have changed everything for our family.

Like everything else in life, things are going to change over time. As the seasons of our lives change, the rituals should change too. The rituals I just described are great for my current season of life. They are very different from our rituals five years ago, and I'm sure our rituals five years from now will be very different too. And that's OK. It's not about doing a certain thing at Mass. It's about being able to contribute everything you've got.

Exercise:

What rituals do you have when it comes to attending Mass? How could your rituals enhance your Sunday experience?

Our lives change when our habits change.

Additional Resources

What the Church, the Bible, and the Saints Teach
Us About the Sacrament of Marriage

Unconditional Love

God's love for his people, the Church, is unconditional. When we love one another, we follow in the image of Christ. And we seek to imitate that unconditional love when we enter the sacrament of marriage. That's why this famous reading in the following Scripture from St. Paul is used so often at weddings.

CATECHISM

1648 It can seem difficult, even impossible, to bind oneself for life to another human being. This makes it all the more important to proclaim the Good News that God loves us with a definitive and irrevocable love, that married couples share in this love, that it supports and sustains them, and that by their own faithfulness they can be witnesses to God's faithful love. Spouses who with God's grace give this witness, often in very difficult conditions, deserve the gratitude and support of the ecclesial community.

SCRIPTURE

If I speak in the tongues of mortals and of angels, but do not have love, I am a noisy gong or a clanging cymbal. And if I have prophetic powers, and understand all mysteries and all knowledge, and if I have all faith, so as to remove mountains, but do not have love, I am nothing. If I give away all my possessions, and if I hand over my body so that I may boast, but do not have love, I gain nothing.

Love is patient; love is kind; love is not envious or boastful or arrogant or rude. It does not insist on its own way; it is not irritable or resentful; it does not rejoice in wrongdoing, but rejoices in the truth. It bears all things, believes all things, hopes all things, endures all things.

Love never ends. But as for prophecies, they will come to an end; as for tongues, they will cease; as for knowledge, it will come to an end. For we know only in part, and we prophesy only in part; but when the complete comes, the partial will come to an end. When I was a child, I spoke like a child, I thought like a child, I reasoned like a child; when I became an adult, I put an end to childish ways. For now we see in a mirror, dimly, but then we will see face to face. Now I know only in part; then I will know fully, even as I have been fully known. And now faith, hope, and love abide, these three; and the greatest of these is love. (1 Corinthians 13)

SAINT

You looked with love upon me and deep within your eyes imprinted grace.
—St. John of the Cross

Notes

Marriage is a coming together for better
or for worse, hopefully enduring, and
intimate to the degree of being sacred.

—**William O. Douglas**

Sexuality

SESSION 7

Wisdom for the Bedroom from Jill

Jill was our family friend for most of my life. Shortly after my father died, I saw her again for the first time in several years when she came to visit my mother.

Jill lives by herself now. Her husband suffered for years from a chronic debilitating illness. In those years of decline, she served him generously and courageously. In his last few months, he was moved into a nursing facility for around-the-clock care. Each day, Jill would sit with him in his room for most of the day, visiting while he was awake, knitting when he slept.

While we were chatting, I asked Jill about caring for her husband for so many years and what stood out in her mind about her noble service to him as he died. She replied, "I think he knew he was going to die on the day he did. I sat with him in his room and we were reminiscing about our fifty years of marriage. He looked at me and asked, 'Honey, will you just lie next to me in the bed here for a few minutes?' So I got in the nursing home bed alongside him, and we held each other for a little while.

"We reminisced about the first bed we shared after our marriage. It was just a twin bed. And we laughed and remembered that tiny bed and those days so long ago."

"After ten or fifteen minutes, I kissed him and got out of the nursing home bed and drove home for the evening."

"About two in the morning, the nursing home called to share with me that he had had a heart attack and died. I think he knew the end was near. I think that's why he wanted just to lie next to each other in the bed one last time. Just to share that closeness. It was so special."

Jill's precious memory stirred something deep in me about the dignity and meaning of a marriage that lasts a lifetime. One filled with highs and lows. One rooted in a deep love, friendship, and affection for each other and for God. In a way, the final experience she and her husband shared captures the very spirit of Hebrews 13:4: "Let marriage be held in honor by all, and let the marriage bed be kept undefiled. . ."

Science actually contradicts one of the great lies of our culture.

_____

Sexuality

7.1
7.2
7.3
7.4
7.5

How to Have a Great Sex Life

The culture wants you to think it's all about sex. Sex, sex, sex—everywhere you go, the culture is talking about it. Have as much as you want, with whomever you want, whenever you want. You can never have enough sex.

That's because the culture thinks sex will make you happy. The culture lies to you and says that sex is the goal. The culture confuses sex with intimacy. But sex is not the goal. Sex can enrich intimacy, but it most certainly is not intimacy. Sex merely contributes to it.

It's important to say two things up front. First, sex is good. After all, God created it. He made us for each other. Sex is a wonderful gift. Second, a good sex life with your spouse will deepen and enhance your marriage and relationship. We all desire to know someone deeply and to be known fully. A good sex life can help make that intimacy a reality. After all, sex is one expression of the love in your marriage.

God wants you to experience deep intimacy in all the forms you can—physically, spiritually, emotionally, and intellectually. He wants you and your mate to be able to share and reveal yourselves to each other throughout your entire marriage. Sex is just one part of that. It can help lead to and deepen the intimacy you share in your marriage.

If you want to have a great sex life in marriage, you need to know five things. While the culture would tell you it's all about fantasies and techniques, that could not be further from the truth. The five things that lead to a great sex life are all about you and your relationship. Get these things right and the rest will take care of itself.

The culture confuses sex with intimacy.

1. **GREAT FRIENDSHIP**

   Just like your marriage, great sex is rooted in friendship. The person who said, "Marry your best friend," was correct. Couples who have a great sex life nurture and sustain their friendship. And they do this over time. They have fun together. They enjoy being with each other and confiding in each other. They play together. They seek each other out because that's what good friends do. This is the foundation for intimacy.

2. **SEX HAS PRIORITY**

   It's easy for sex to get lost in the whirlwind. Schedules get busy. Lives become full. The to-do list grows longer and longer. Humans are tired at the end of the day. When all these things naturally occur, it is easy to let sex slide. It's also easy to neglect your friendship. A great sex life means that sex is a priority in your marriage. It is not merely something else we need to do on our list, or something we will do if everything else on the list gets done first. Your sex life must be a priority.

3. **BE TRANSPARENT**

   Couples who enjoy a great sex life value honest conversation. They can talk openly about sex with each other. They do not avoid the subject or clam up when the conversation turns to this dimension of their relationship. Your spouse is not a mind reader; he cannot know you unless you reveal yourself to him and vice versa. Great couples share their feelings and their hopes with each other. Honesty and openness prevail because each spouse wants to know deeply and be deeply known.

4. **KEEP DATING**

   All marriages benefit from continuing to date (each other; it's probably important to note that!). And this is especially true for spouses who want to cultivate a great sex life. Husband and wife spend regular time together. They enjoy the carefree timelessness of a date. Long walks. Wandering conversations. Movies. Hikes. Holding hands. Time together. The dating

KEEP DATING

One thing that was super helpful in my marriage once I had kids was the awareness that "dating" didn't have to mean going to dinner and a movie. My wife and I could wait to eat until after the kids went to bed, make a nice meal together, leave the TV off and put the cell phones upstairs, light a candle while we ate, sit next to each other, and that could be an excellent date night. It was important because it helped us realize that a weekly date night was possible as a couple with kids, as long as we didn't limit ourselves to a super strict definition of "date."

—Dominick,
   Dynamic Catholic Ambassador

maintains the spark and strengthens the friendship and the intimacy. Couples guard and protect their time together.

5.   **SHOW AFFECTION**

Couples who have a great sex life show affection for each other. And they do so in public as well as in private. The husband holds his wife's hand. The wife places her hand on her husband. They sit near each other. They also snuggle and cuddle in private. Affection plays a central and natural role in their marriage and bolsters their sexual relationship.

One of the great gifts of marriage given by God is the gift of sexual intimacy. That gift, shared with one other person within your marriage, is a beautiful thing.

Exercise:

Sit together and hold hands for five minutes. Nothing more, nothing less. Just enjoy the intimacy and connection that is established in that simple act.

....
....
....
....
....
....
....
....
....
....
....
....
....
....

Sexuality

7.1

7.2

7.3

7.4

7.5

How to Have a Bad Sex Life

No one wants a bad sex life. To lose attraction to each other. To feel frustrated. To see some of the intimacy in the marriage withering. To feel unloved or not known.

But the truth is, that does happen. And it happens to good people and good couples. And many of them never see it coming.

Usually couples who experience a bad sex life exhibit one key characteristic in their relationships. And it may surprise you just how simple that one thing is: They fail to be intentional about seeking each other out.

We're not just talking about seeking each other out sexually. The problem runs far deeper than that. Marriages with struggles in their sex life are often the result of the fact that the husband and wife spend very little time together. They get preoccupied with their jobs, their responsibilities as parents, their own dreams or interests, or their ever-growing to-do lists. And all too often, selfishness sets in. The single greatest enemy of a great sex life is selfishness.

It's easy for this to happen. Life is busy. And life is messy.

Couples who experience bad sex lives usually fail to pull themselves above the daily busyness and make each other a priority. Rather than their mate, their relationship, and their sex life being priorities, everything else takes precedence. So many other things are important that the relationship itself gets taken for granted. They just assume it will drive itself. But it doesn't.

Slowly but steadily, the woman and man drift apart. Not intentionally. No, it's much more insidious than that. They just are not paying much attention, like a driver texting as she makes her way down the road. Not really noticing the curves in the road or the painted lines in the middle. Swerving a little here, running off the berm there, and occasionally running a red light that just went unnoticed. Soon, she fails to make the turn she needs to go in the right direction. So busy with her texting and other things, she fails to notice that she

God unites husband and wife so closely in himself, that it should be easier to sunder soul from body than husband from wife.

—St. Francis de Sales

no longer has any idea where she is. Or worse, she fails to notice that her car is running into the ditch. Until it's too late.

Most car accidents are caused by drivers failing to pay attention. A large percentage of struggling marriages are caused by the spouses failing to pay attention and failing to make their relationship a priority. A bad sex life almost always is the result of a relationship in which everything is a priority except the relationship itself.

There is no cultivation of friendship. No dating. No honest conversation because there is just no time for it. No priority for sex because the to-do list and other stuff are too much. And no affection for each other because our minds are elsewhere. There's just so much to do.

When there is no intentional seeking each other out, the temptation for many people is to retreat into pornography. They create a secluded virtual world all to themselves, where no one else is welcome. A world that is all about them and their own wants and fantasies, where everything is perfect. Because it is just in the mind. It is not real.

Tragically, porn kills a great sex life. The culture says porn makes sex great. But it does just the opposite. **Porn isn't about love; it's about fantasy and lust.** Porn destroys intimacy because it is fundamentally self-centered. Love gives; porn gets. Porn invites strangers and fiction into one of the most intimate areas of your marriage. And in the end, porn excludes your spouse because it is all about you.

No driver sets out to get lost. No driver ever wants to land in the ditch. But when we are distracted, unintentional, and focused on the wrong things, bad things happen.

The same is true for your marriage and relationship. And it is also absolutely true for your sex life.

When you fail to be intentional about seeking each other out—to spend time together, to talk, to hold hands, to simply to be together, to know and be known—it only makes sense that the first thing to go will be your sex life. And nobody ever wants that.

Discover ways that porn destroys love and prevents great sex. Discover excellent resources to prevent that from happening in your marriage at Fight the New Drug: **fightthenewdrug.org**

With all vigilance guard your heart, for in it are the sources of life.

(Proverbs 4:23)

Sexuality

7.1

7.2

7.3

7.4

7.5

Protect Your Wife from All Harm

Your marriage will face challenges.

Many of those challenges will revolve around your health or your partner's health and will not be your fault. A diagnosis of cancer. Struggles with infertility. An accident that disables you or your mate.

But some health challenges are preventable. For example, as a man, if you knew that eating at a particular restaurant once a week increased the chance of your wife getting breast cancer by as much as 38 percent, would you let her eat there? Probably not. Because you would want to protect her health.

Men, what would you say if you discovered that doing one thing increased suicide risk in your wife by 300 percent[1], increased her risk of depression by up to 34 percent[2], and did in fact increase her risk of breast cancer by as much as 38 percent[3]? You would want to know what that one thing was and help protect your wife from it. You're a man. That's what we do.

Here's that one thing: taking hormonal birth control.

Science actually contradicts one of the great lies of our culture: that using hormonal birth control is completely safe and healthy.

---

1 Skovlund, Charlotte Wessel, Ph.D., Lina Steinrud Mørch, Ph.D., Lars Vedel Kessing, D.M.Sc., Theis Lange, Ph.D., and Øjvind Lidegaard, D.M.Sc. "Association of Hormonal Contraception With Suicide Attempts and Suicides." *American Journal of Psychiatry* 175, no. 4 (November 2017): 336-42.

2 Skovlund, Charlotte Wessel, M.Sc., Lina Steinrud Mørch, Ph.D., Lars Vedel Kessing, M.D., DM.Sc., and Øjvind Lidegaard, M.D., DM.Sc. "Association of Hormonal Contraception With Depression." *JAMA Psychiatry* 73, no. 11 (November 1, 2016): 1154-162.

3 Lina S. Mørch, Ph.D. et al., "Contemporary Hormonal Contraception and the Risk of Breast Cancer," *The New England Journal of Medicine* 377, no. 23 (December 7, 2017): 2228-239.

For women, the evidence shows it clearly is not. In addition to the risk factors mentioned here, scientific studies also point to increased risks of heart attack, cervical cancer, and high blood pressure. In fact, my own aunt died from a stroke related to her use of the pill. Tragically, and paradoxically, research also indicates that the use of hormonal birth control increases the risk of infertility.

When you think about it, it makes sense. Consider it from a natural point of view. Imposing synthetic hormones on your natural system is bound to mess with your desire for clean living and organic well-being. It seems kind of obvious, doesn't it?

The culture does not like you to know, but when researchers were working on the creation of hormonal contraception, women died during the female tests, and men's testicles radically shrank during the male tests[4]. But the researchers kept going, stopped the development process for hormonal birth control for men, and focused exclusively on women.

As a man, as the protector of your wife, if you encourage her to take the pill, what does that say about you?

Marriage is all about my giving my whole self to you as your spouse. I give you my heart, my soul, my mind, my emotions, my finances, and my body—my whole self, in every way.

But what would you think if I told you before we got married, "I am giving you my whole self but on Friday nights I want to go out with my old girlfriend. We're not gonna have sex or anything. I just kind of miss her and I like hanging out with her now and then."

You'd think I was nuts. You'd also think I was not serious about

---

4 Jonathan Eig, *The Birth of the Pill: How Four Crusaders Reinvented Sex and Launched a Revolution.* London, England: Pan Books, 2016.

really giving you my whole self. You'd think that I was holding back part of myself from you. Using contraception is like that. I'm not giving you my whole self. And we are not allowing God to have center stage in our marriage. In many ways, we are refusing to let God be God. This is part of why the Church teaches what it does about contraception.

Marriage is hard enough to begin with. But when we hold back part of ourselves and impose barriers to God in our relationship, we are making it even harder.

Are you open to the idea that there is a better way than the culture offers? If you are, I invite you to take a look at the resources included in this book.

If you are, I invite you to take a look at how one doctor approaches the health and well-being of women.

Visit **DynamicCatholic.com/WomensHealth**

What does love look like? It has the hands to help others.

—St. Augustine of Hippo

Great Expectations

Slothfulness creates disinterest. It's true for your appetites. If you eat filet mignon every day, after a while, you cannot even taste the food anymore. If you just eat whatever you want whenever you want, throw some stuff into the microwave, slop it down, pretty soon you lose any sense of pleasure or experience when you eat. You don't even notice what you're eating, remember what you ate, or enjoy the process at all. Slothfulness creates disinterest.

When you bring discipline to your life, you actually keep desire alive and you keep appreciation thriving. It is true for your appetites. Not having what you want whenever you want it actually makes you more alive.

No Olympic athlete ever won a medal without discipline. No investor ever became wealthy without discipline. No writer ever completed a book without discipline. No student ever earned a degree without discipline. And no person ever got healthy without discipline. Discipline is hated by our culture. But it is also our best friend. The only way to become the-best-version-of-yourself is to embrace discipline.

And the same thing is true for your sexual appetite. The culture has lied to you. Having sex however you want, whenever you want, with whomever you want only leads to appreciating and enjoying it less. And it doesn't lead to more intimacy. It doesn't even lead to less intimacy. It actually leads to *no* intimacy. You're just going through the motions, trying to satisfy some physical desire or psychological want, and the more you do it, the less satisfied you become. Slothfulness leads to disinterest.

It just may be that the key to a great sex life and a satisfying marriage is not doing whatever you want whenever you want it. It just may be that the key is discipline. Because discipline leads to success and fulfillment.

Natural family planning brings discipline to your sexual appetite and desires, and to your marriage. And discipline is your best friend.

The fruit of the Spirit is love, joy, peace, patience, kindness, generosity, faithfulness, gentleness, and self-control.

(Galatians 5:22–23)

When you hear the words *natural family planning*, what do you think? Be honest. Maybe . . .

What in the world is that?

OR

I'm gonna end up with ten kids and how in the world are we ever gonna handle that?

OR

Doing that means we will only have sex, like, three times a year.

OR

If I do that, there is no way I will ever be able to have a career.

OR

Are you kidding me? That is for freaks. Nobody does that.

What would you say if I told you that natural family planning would increase your sex life by twenty years? That's right. Twenty years. By instilling a new level of discipline and appreciation into your relationship.

Natural family planning is a natural, scientific, moral, and safe tool used to help couples achieve or avoid pregnancy. Remarkably, this process actually increases intimacy. Rather than using devices or drugs for birth control, couples who embrace natural family planning learn to read the body's signs of fertility and infertility. In doing so, the husband becomes more involved in understanding his wife's body and how it works. That familiarity actually increases intimacy. And it deepens your relationship and your sex life.

Best of all, natural family planning keeps you open to one of the greatest blessings God could ever give you: a child. The gift of a new life. The miracle of creation. And the discovery of a love beyond compare.

The Church teaches natural family planning for all kinds of reasons: the healthy discipline it brings, the intimacy it fosters, and the openness to new life it provides. It is not just some form of Catholic contraception. Rather, it is a healthy approach to both sex and marriage.

Are you open to the idea that there is a better way than the culture offers? If you are, I invite you to take a look at the resources included in this book.

If you are, I invite you to hear the professional wisdom of a doctor regarding contraception and natural family planning.

Visit **DynamicCatholic.com/FamilyPlanning**

Sexuality

7.1

7.2

7.3

7.4

7.5

God Wants You to Have a Great Sex Life

You've been told all these lies since before you can even remember: God hates sex. The Church is against sex. You are a sexual creature who should do whatever you want whenever you want. Sex will make you happy. Life is all about sex. And the list goes on and on.

But the truth is the Church loves sex and God does too. In fact, God not only wants you to have sex, he wants you to have a great sex life—the best there is. After all, he made us male and female for each other. Sex belongs to him.

Sex offers your marriage the possibility of a connection and depth not available anywhere else. A good sex life can unite you in a unique way known only to a husband and wife. That uniqueness will deepen your intimacy to levels the culture can only begin to dream about. God's dream is for you to discover that there is nothing more intimate than the giving of your whole selves to each other in every aspect of your relationship. Sex deepens and enriches that companionship. It is not intimacy in itself, but it does help make intimacy possible and real in a significant way.

Of course, a great sex life also allows you to be open to the possibilities God has in mind for your marriage. And those possibilities include children. **The gift of children is an outward expression of the love you have for each other.** Children multiply that love and expand it in new ways. And a great sex life cooperates with God in expressing and expanding that love.

As Catholics, we understand children for who they are, in and of themselves:

- Unique expressions of the love between a man and a woman
- Wonderful creations made in the image of God
- Valuable each in their own right

God wants sex to help both of you become the-best-version-of-yourselves. Unity, life, bonding, intimacy, fidelity, love. All of those dimensions open you up to grow in ways you can only begin to imagine right now. Again, God has a greater dream for your life than you can envision on your own. And a great sex life is a part of that.

I invite you to question the lies of the culture. And I invite you to consider what the Church has to offer.

Exercise:

Sit quietly together and have an honest conversation for fifteen minutes about the sex life you want to create as a married couple. What do you most hope for? What are you most afraid of? Be honest. Your honesty will build deeper trust and intimacy.

I have found you, and I intend to give myself totally in order to form a truly Christian family.

—St. Gianna Beretta Molla

———————

I ask you to swim against the tide; yes, I am asking
you to rebel against this culture that sees everything
as temporary and that ultimately believes you are
incapable of responsibility, that believes you are
incapable of true love. I have confidence in you and
I pray for you.

—Pope Francis

Additional Resources

What the Church, the Bible, and the Saints Teach
Us About the Sacrament of Marriage

Sex and Faithfulness

Sexuality comes directly from the mind and heart of God.

The Church endorses the positive beauty of sexuality in marriage. Marital intercourse is "noble and honorable," established by God so that "spouses should experience pleasure and enjoyment of body and spirit" (CCC 2362). In other words, sexuality can help lead to a deep personal unity in every dimension of the marriage: physical, emotional, spiritual, and intellectual.

The Church's understanding of sexuality is rooted in the teachings of Jesus that were often drawn from the wisdom of the Old Testament. For example, the book of Genesis and the Song of Songs both describe the basic goodness of sexual love in marriage.

Marital sexuality achieves two purposes. First, in creating new human life, sometimes called the procreative dimension of sexuality, the couple cooperates with the Creator's love. Second, sexual union expresses and deepens the love between husband and wife. This is called the unitive, or relational, dimension of sexuality.

CATECHISM

1643 Conjugal love involves a totality, in which all the elements of the person enter—appeal of the body and instinct, power of feeling and affectivity, aspiration of the spirit and of will. It aims at a deeply personal unity, a unity that, beyond union in one flesh, leads to forming one heart and soul; it demands *indissolubility* and *faithfulness* in definitive mutual giving; and it is open to *fertility*.

1646 By its very nature conjugal love requires the inviolable fidelity of the spouses. This is the consequence of the gift of themselves which they make to each other. Love seeks to be definitive; it cannot be an arrangement "until further notice." The "intimate union of marriage, as a mutual giving of two persons, and the good of the children, demand total fidelity from the spouses and require an unbreakable union between them."

Procreative and unitive.

You have ravished my heart, my Sister, my Bride;
you have ravished my heart with one glance of your eyes,
with one hair on your neck.

How beautiful are your breasts, my Sister, my Bride;
how much more delightful are your breasts than wine
and the fragrance of your ointments than all spices!

Sweetness drips from your lips, O Bride;
honey and milk are under your tongue,
and the scent of your robes is like the scent of Lebanon.

You are an enclosed garden, my Sister, my Bride,
an enclosed garden, a fountain sealed.
You are a park that puts forth pomegranates
with all choice fruits, with henna, with spikenard,
with nard and saffron, calamus and cinnamon, with all the trees of Lebanon,
with myrrh and aloes and all the finest spices.
You are a garden fountain, a well of living water,
flowing fresh from Lebanon.
(Song of Songs 4:9–15 Trans: Fr. Basil Pennington, OCSO)

Every man and every woman fully realizes himself or herself through the sincere gift of self. For spouses, the moment of conjugal union constitutes a very particular expression of this. It is then that a man and woman, in the "truth" of their masculinity and femininity, become a mutual gift to each other. All married life is a gift; but this becomes most evident when the spouses, in giving themselves to each other in love, bring about that encounter which makes them "one flesh."
—St. John Paul II, "Letter to Families," 12

Love begins by taking care of the closest

ones—the ones at home.

—St. Teresa of Calcutta

Family

SESSION 8

Wisdom for Generous Love from Beth and Lou

I went to the business seminar not expecting much. In general, I dread professional workshops. But when I heard the wisdom of the Holtz marriage from Lou, one of the speakers, I wrote it down. It was too good not to keep and use in my own marriage and family.

Beth Holtz had birthed four children, welcomed nine grandchildren, and been married to Lou Holtz for forty-eight years when she developed stage four cancer. She endured thirteen hours of surgery, eighty-three radiation treatments, and enormous suffering.

Her children and grandchildren organized themselves to care for her and encourage her. Drives to the doctor's office, meals, visits, prayers, cards, gifts. In short, they rallied around their mother and grandmother, who had selflessly and generously served them and other people for decades.

When the storm had passed, and she had survived the cancer, a reporter asked Beth, "What's the most important thing you learned from having cancer?"

She replied, "I learned how much my family loves me."

When her husband, Lou, heard that, he realized, "It's not that we loved her more; it's just that we actually showed it."

Sacrificial love.

_____

The proof of love is in the works. Where love exists, it works great things. But when it ceases to act, it ceases to exist.

—St. Gregory the Great

Family
gives your
life roots.

___

Family

8.1
8.2
8.3
8.4
8.5

Know Your Stories

Everyone thinks the way they grew up is normal. We all assume that the way life was for us was the same for most of the people around us. Sometimes we make this assumption consciously and sometimes it is bubbling underneath the surface and we are not really aware of it.

Think for a moment about what your life was like growing up. What was your family like? What was it like to be a kid in your house?

> I grew up in a traditional home—my dad was the breadwinner and my mom stayed home to raise my sister and me. There wasn't much visible conflict in our home—voices weren't raised, and it was always important to be socially gracious no matter what. At times, this dynamic meant that things looked good on the surface, but also meant that some important things weren't discussed. It definitely led me to stuff a lot of feelings, and I didn't see conflict modeled in a healthy way. I think that my parents were genuinely pretty happy, but not having ever seen much disagreement meant that I wasn't sure how to handle it when I got married.

This story of your family is important to think about for a lot of reasons. First, we tend to re-create what we know. Kids who grow up with faithful Catholic parents are more likely to grow up to be faithful Catholics. Children who have an alcoholic parent(s) are more likely to become alcoholics than kids who did not grow up with an alcoholic. Kids from divorced families have a higher probability of becoming divorced themselves than children whose parents stayed married.

Obviously, these tendencies are not absolute. You get to decide what kind of family you want to create. But the trend is important to be aware of. Again, we tend to re-create what we know. In other words, we often form the same kind of family we grew up in. If you want to create something different, it is important to think about that up front, now. That way, you can take the steps and make the decisions to create the kind of family you and your partner dream of.

The second reason your family story is important is because your background tends not to stay in the background. Your family of origin and your home life have not only shaped who you are now, but they will keep on shaping you into the future. If your home life was full of chaos all the time, that lack of stability still informs how you react to situations and respond to people. You can still hear some of the memories and people from your background sitting in the balcony of your head, speaking into what you are doing right now. The more aware you become of this, the more you can develop healthy habits with your mate to recognize what each of you is bringing from your past and your family into your new life together.

The story of your past helps define who you are today. Knowing each other's stories well can help you dream and make the choices to determine who you will be as individuals and as a couple beginning tomorrow.

Everyone thinks how they grew up is normal. And your way is normal. . . for you.

So think about the questions again. What was your life like growing up? What was your family like? What was it like to be a kid in your house?

To hear more wisdom from our contributors, go to
DynamicCatholic.com/ViewProgram

215

Reflect:

What were a few things that surprised you about your spouse's family of origin stories? What new things did you learn?

....

....

....

....

....

....

....

....

....

....

....

....

....

....

....

....

....

....

....

....

....

....

Exercise:

Share your family story with your betrothed.

What was your life like growing up?

What was your family like?

What kinds of traditions did your family have?

What was important in your family? What was never important?

What was it like to be a kid in your house?

How was discipline handled?

What was your father like? Your mother? Your siblings?

....

....

....

....

....

....

....

....

....

....

....

....

....

....

....

....

....

....

....

....

....

....

....

Family

8.1

8.2

8.3

8.4

8.5

Your Family Dream

God has a dream for your family. The two of you are creating something new, something that has never existed before. You now know each other's stories, and you get to create your own story together. The two of you are becoming one—one new family and home base together. You are co-creators with God.

What do you think God's dream for your family is? One of the ways to discover it is to discuss together your own dreams for your family. Remember from Session 2 that one of the most powerful experiences any person can have is to share a dream with someone, articulate it clearly, and then pursue it passionately together. Shared dreams give energy and life to your marriage.

God has a vision for your family. He didn't create us to be alone. The family is the foundation of civilization; it is the basic building block of any stable society. If you want to predict the future of a society, watch the direction families are moving in that society. Are families becoming more stable or more chaotic? Is there more love or more disarray in them?

You and I initially experience the love of God in our first community of love—our family. Your family was and is your first experience of not being alone. It is your first experience of love, whether positive or negative. Family gives your life roots, a home base.

Never underestimate how deep those roots are and how strong the draw of family is. The bond is so strong that even it if is tattered and unhealthy, children nevertheless feel the bond and are pulled back to it. Family is our roots. The older we get, the more we think about our roots. In a healthy family, we are loved and accepted regardless of what we have done, what we have, or who we are in the world's eyes. Family, like love, is built on acceptance.

Even children from the most dysfunctional of homes—families filled with addictions, poor choices, and chaos—still feel a deep and powerful attraction back to those roots.

Family provides the primary cell or foundation for the Church, just as it does for society. If we learn the faith at home, we have our greatest chance to thrive. The family becomes our community, where we help each other become the-best-version-of-ourselves. And lots of wonderful things come with that: love, boundaries, safety, correction, encouragement, and accountability.

So as you think about the family, as you dream, consider it from the positive perspective first. What are some things or qualities that you definitely want in your family? Perhaps you want a family in which the parents stay together no matter what. Or one that prays together regularly. Or a family that rides horses together. Or maybe you really desire a family in which the husband and wife take traditional roles.

Then dream about your family from the opposite perspective. What are some things or qualities that you definitely do not want in your family? Sometimes we are clearer about that than we are about what we do want. For example, my mother grew up with an alcoholic father and she knew from the beginning that she absolutely wanted a husband who did not drink at all. This was important to her. She knew her background, and that shaped what she wanted, so she took steps to ensure she wouldn't end up with an alcoholic home. Or maybe you want a home in which no one screams at each other. What are some things that you definitely do not want?

family, like love, is built on acceptance.

Discuss:

What are some things or qualities that you definitely want in your family? What are some things or qualities that you definitely do not want in your family?

....
....
....
....
....
....
....
....
....
....
....
....
....
....
....
....
....
....
....
....
....
....
....
....
....
....
....
....

Everything comes from love, all is ordained for the salvation of man, God does nothing without this goal in mind.

—St. Catherine of Siena

Family

8.1

8.2

8.3

8.4

8.5

The Greatest Gift You Can Give Your Family

Storms will arrive in different ways for every family. The question is not if the storm is coming, but when. Disagreements about where you will live, the anguish of a diagnosis of illness for you or your child, the loss of a job and the stability it provided. When storms appear, deep roots will make all the difference in the world. Trees with deep roots weather the storm.

The greatest gift you can give your children and your family is a strong marriage. You and your spouse form the nucleus of your cell, the centerpiece of your family. If the two of you remain healthy and strong as a team, your family will experience the consistency and vitality that brings. Your love and health will breathe love and health into your children and the whole family. Your strength will be their strength. You will be the deep roots of your family.

So how are you going to care for your marriage? How are you going to care for each other so that you keep the center strong, so that the roots grow deep and firm? I have already mentioned the significance of praying as individuals, as a couple, and as a family in Session 6. And an entire session will be devoted to how to get better every day in your marriage in Session 11.

But now is a good time to begin reflecting on the question. How are you going to care for your marriage? Because it will not be as easy as it seems right now.

Seasons of life change. Seasons of marriage change. And different seasons bring different challenges, different storms. And those different seasons expose where your relationship is strong and where it is vulnerable.

Kevin did not anticipate how much his life and family would change when his father was diagnosed with cancer. As the disease grew and spread, Kevin found himself doing more and more to care for his father. And he also found his time increasingly devoted to helping his mother cope with seeing her husband of forty-seven years bedridden and assuming all the responsibilities that go with a terminally ill spouse. For three years, Kevin devoted most of his energy to helping his parents. He and his wife, Lucy, did not even notice how little energy they were investing in each other; they just got swept up in Kevin caring for his parents and Lucy taking everything on herself at their own home. But once Kevin's father died, Kevin and Lucy discovered that they had grown apart in ways that they never would have guessed during these three years of stress. Their season of life had changed, and they had not been paying careful attention to each other in the midst of it. Their old habits of a weekly date night, a morning prayer together, and spending several evenings each week taking a long walk and just talking had all disappeared under the strain of responsibilities each had taken on. It took time to restore intimacy, familiarity, and genuine care for each other after neglecting each other for so long. Seasons change, and with that, how you care for your marriage will change too.

Keeping those roots strong will require different things in different seasons. What works for you now may not be the same thing that keeps your relationship strong when you have children, or when you are empty-nesters after many years filled with the needs of kids, or even when you are retired and work no longer occupies most of your mind and time.

As you spend time in the classroom of silence and prayer, you will learn to listen for the Holy Spirit speaking in your life. Your self-awareness will grow in prayer as you enter new seasons in your life and marriage. Invite the Holy Spirit to help you navigate through those changes together. No one ever relied too much on the Holy Spirit. How will you rely on him together in your marriage?

No one ever relied too much on the Holy Spirit.

Exercise:

What is one thing you feel God saying to you in this section?

....

....

....

....

....

....

....

....

....

....

....

....

....

....

....

....

....

....

....

....

....

....

....

....

....

....

....

....

....

....

When husband and wife are united in marriage they no longer seem like something earthly, but rather like the image of God Himself.

—St. John Chrysostom

Family

8.1

8.2

8.3

8.4

8.5

A Vision for Your Kids

You probably know the saying "Begin with the end in mind." And you probably know its first cousin, "If you don't know where you're going, you will probably end up someplace else."

When it comes to having children, those two sayings are truer than ever before.

With children, we spend so much time living in the moment that we miss asking the big question: What is our goal here? Or, what is the end we have in mind?

Children ask why about everything. But adults and parents rarely do.
Why do we want them to play soccer?
Why do we want our son to go to this school?
Why does our daughter love to spend so much time reading when we really want her to practice the piano?

At some point, we get so deep and so far into something that we realize no one ever asked why we were doing it in the first place. Why are we doing this?

Daniel and Rebekah spent most of their time taking their eldest child, Robert, to soccer practice, paying for his lessons, and traveling on weekends to his tournaments. All of Robert's friends and their families were doing the travel soccer adventure, so Daniel and Rebekah just joined right in. It cost a lot of money to pay for all the lessons and the travel, so Daniel picked up an extra job as a security officer at night. The travel took a lot of time, and their two younger children, Christopher and Elizabeth, really did not appreciate following Robert across the country to watch his soccer games. But they did it because their parents told them to do it. After all, Robert was good at soccer, and he was the oldest, so the habits formed early. Plus, Daniel and Rebekah hoped that he might be good enough to get a scholarship to college one day.

Since they traveled most weekends to tournaments, the family rarely went to Mass. They were on the road and preoccupied with other stuff. And soccer practices took place three evenings a week, which meant the family rarely participated in their parish. They just had a lot going on. And all their friends were doing the same thing.

No one in the family ever asked, "Why are we doing this?" No one ever thought about what they were really trying to achieve. And so, after a few years of this, a number of things began to happen that Daniel and Rebekah had never anticipated.

- Robert got burned out on soccer. He had been doing so much of it from such an early age that he never developed other areas of his life. He became one-dimensional and got sick of the one thing he always seemed to be doing: soccer.
- Christopher and Elizabeth grew resentful. They had been dragged along week after week. Neither of them had ever really been given much of an opportunity to explore and grow their own passions and interests. They felt neglected and stunted.
- The family felt disconnected spiritually. They had no parish community and no sense of roots. They failed to do any-thing with their faith besides the bare minimum of dropping the kids off at the First Communion preparation to get that marked off the to-do list.

Daniel and Rebekah did not mean for these things to happen. They just never stopped to ask, "What are we doing and why are we do-ing it?" And as a result, so many decisions got made for the wrong reasons. Without intending to do so, they had inadvertently put soccer and Robert at the center of their family and had nudged God out altogether.

Families do this all the time. Make decisions for the wrong reasons. They send little Johnny to this school because that is where Grand-pa went and they want to keep that tradition. Never mind that the school doesn't really fit what Johnny needs for his development. They enroll Catherine in ballet lessons year after year because Mommy loved ballet and wants that for her daughter too. She never notices that Catherine sits on the side of the room, rarely engages with the teacher, and never practices on her own. Because Catherine hates ballet.

Knowing why is important. Why are you doing what you are doing? As parents you are responsible for your child's education, growth in virtue, extracurricular activities, and spiritual formation, just to name a few. It's a huge role. You're not a babysitter; babysitters merely prevent death. Parents grow and develop a human being made in the image of God. Intentionality is your best friend.

The lifelong habits you help instill in your child can make all the difference in the world. Mass is a lifelong habit; prayer is a lifelong habit. These habits start young and will provide the roots for your child to weather any storms that come.

A good way to begin is by envisioning your child as she reaches age 12, then age 21, and finally, age 45. What do you hope she will be? Who do you hope she will be? A hard worker, a wise decision maker, a confident and loyal friend, a faithful Catholic?

Ask that question, and get really clear on it. Then parent to that vision. Make the decisions along the way about education and activities that help fulfill that vision.

What are you doing and why are you doing it? Having a clear vision of your purpose is an excellent place to start.

Begin with the end in mind.

Exercise:

Envision and describe your child at age 12, age 21, age 45.

What's your vision? What do you definitely want and definitely not want them to be or have at those ages? Who does God want them to be at those ages?

Getting clear on this will help you parent toward that vision and make decisions well along the way.

Notes

Family

8.1

8.2

8.3

8.4

8.5

The Greatest Gift God Can Give You

There is no way anyone can discuss everything about parenting. But I can provide you with a basic governing principle.

Have a basic governing principle. This will give you a center. There will be countless little decisions along the way as you grow your family and rear your children. You can make those decisions quickly, on impulse, without much thought. Or you can be intentional. With a governing principle, you can ask questions about what is best and what is not, about what matters most and what matters least. That way, no matter what decisions you face as a parent or as a family, you can come back to the principle to guide you.

Here it is: **Prepare your child for the road and not the road for your child.**

There will be times you want to control too much. When those times arise, remember this principle.

There will be times you want to do too little. When you do, again remember this principle.

Prepare your child for the road. When your child reaches adulthood, you will want him to be independent and mature, capable of caring for himself and for others, prepared to make decisions and accept the consequences. And his road of life will be rocky. Your child will face challenges and obstacles. You will want him to learn how to persevere through hardships, not throw up his hands and quit. You will want him to find solutions to problems, not whine and complain. You will want to help him develop a healthy work ethic and perseverance, not micromanage his grades. You will want him to have healthy relationships, not self-centered ones. In sum, you want your child not to be some second-rate, weak, dependent, whiny version of himself. You want him to be the-best-version-of-himself and nothing short of that. That is God's dream and it is your dream too.

Along the way, you will be tempted to cushion him from the pain of failure or disappointment, and occasionally you will want to entirely prevent failure or disappointment. But there will be times you need to let your son experience the consequences of his decisions or his performance.

You will need to make decisions about discipline. You will have to choose what you approve of and what you don't. You will face choices about your child's friends and who he spends time with. As you make those decisions, keep in mind how you want to prepare your child for the road.

Storms will come and you want your child to be ready when they do.

Adulthood will come and you want your child to be ready when it does.

With a governing principle in mind to come back to, you will be preparing your child for the road. And you will avoid the all-too-common mistake of weakening your child by trying to prepare the road, which leads to entitlement, self-absorption, poor work ethic, and lack of responsibility and accountability. You have lived or worked with people who embody all those things, and you do not want your child to be one of them.

So here it is, your basic governing principle for parenting: Prepare your child for the road and not the road for your child.

Embrace that, and rely on the Holy Spirit to help you and guide you. In the end, you will have given your child all that he or she could ever hope for.

Pray Together

May the strength of God pilot us.
May the power of God preserve us.
May the wisdom of God instruct us.
May the hand of God protect us.
May the way of God direct us.
May the shield of God defend us.
May the host of God guard us
Against the snares of the evil ones,
Against temptations of the world.
May Christ be with us!
Christ above us!
Christ in us,
Christ before us.
May thy salvation, Lord,
Always be ours,
This day, O Lord, and evermore.

—St. Patrick – Celtic Benediction

Additional Resources

What the Church, the Bible, and the Saints Teach
Us About the Sacrament of Marriage

The Supreme Gift

Love is life-giving. It pours out generously. The mutual love of a married couple is designed by God to be open to new life.

The power to create a child with God is at the heart of what spouses share with each other in sexual intercourse. Mutual love includes the mutual gift of fertility. Couples who are not able to conceive or who are beyond their childbearing years can still express openness to life. They can share their generative love with grandchildren, other children and families, and the wider community.

The family arises from marriage. Parents, children, and family members form what is called a domestic church, or church of the home. This is the primary unit of the Church—the place where the Church lives in the daily love, care, hospitality, sacrifice, forgiveness, prayer, and faith of ordinary families.

Love is
life-giving.

1652 "By its very nature the institution of marriage and married love is ordered to the procreation and education of the offspring and it is in them that it finds its crowning glory."

Children are the supreme gift of marriage and contribute greatly to the good of the parents themselves. God himself said: "It is not good that man should be alone," and "from the beginning [he] made them male and female"; wishing to associate them in a special way in his own creative work, God blessed man and woman with the words: "Be fruitful and multiply." Hence, true married love and the whole structure of family life which results from it, without diminishment of the other ends of marriage, are directed to disposing the spouses to cooperate valiantly with the love of the Creator and Savior, who through them will increase and enrich his family from day to day.

1653 The fruitfulness of conjugal love extends to the fruits of the moral, spiritual, and supernatural life that parents hand on to their children by education. Parents are the principal and first educators of their children. In this sense the fundamental task of marriage and family is to be at the service of life.

1654 Spouses to whom God has not granted children can nevertheless have a conjugal life full of meaning, in both human and Christian terms. Their marriage can radiate a fruitfulness of charity, of hospitality, and of sacrifice.

1655 Christ chose to be born and grow up in the bosom of the holy family of Joseph and Mary. The Church is nothing other than "the family of God." From the beginning, the core of the Church was often constituted by those who had become believers "together with all [their] household." When they were converted, they desired that "their whole household" should also be saved. These families who became believers were islands of Christian life in an unbelieving world.

1656 In our own time, in a world often alien and even hostile to faith, believing families are of primary importance as centers of living, radiant faith. For this reason the Second Vatican Council, using an ancient expression, calls the family the *Ecclesia domestica*. It is in the bosom of the family that parents are "by word and example. . . the first heralds of the faith with regard to their children. They should encourage them in the vocation which is proper to each child, fostering with special care any religious vocation.

1657 It is here that the father of the family, the mother, children, and all members of the family exercise the *priesthood of the baptized* in a privileged way "by the reception of the sacraments, prayer and thanksgiving, the witness of a holy life, and self-denial and active charity." Thus the home is the first school of Christian life and "a school for human enrichment." Here one learns endurance and the joy of work, fraternal love, generous—even repeated—forgiveness, and above all divine worship in prayer and the offering of one's life.

SCRIPTURE

Now the man knew his wife Eve, and she conceived and bore Cain, saying, "I have produced a man with the help of the Lord."
(Genesis 4:1)

SAINT

Saints Joachim and Anne helped each other become saints as a married couple. How did they do that? By welcoming and nourishing the remarkable gift of their child, Mary, the Mother of God.

To get the full value of joy you must have someone to divide it with.

—**Mark Twain**

Money

SESSION 9

Wisdom for Oneness from Pat and Helen

My wife and I met Pat and Helen a week after we got married. We lived not far from them and were part of the same church. We needed a mentor couple to inspire us, and Pat and Helen did just that for the first three years of our marriage. Their rich wisdom has fueled our marriage ever since.

Married for more than fifty years when we first met them, Pat and Helen lived modest lives. He had been a construction worker and manager; she served as a librarian for many years before retiring. They had three grown children, all boys, who had families of their own.

In their retirement, Pat and Helen did everything together. They walked together. They read together. They volunteered at their church together. They ate nearly every meal together. Most of all, they gardened together.

It is hard to say whether Pat or Helen enjoyed gardening more. Either way, their garden was the envy of the community. Not too large but not too small, it prospered every year under their care. They grew tomatoes and squash, some corn and some beans, and a host of other vegetables that they generously served up on their dinner table for guests as well as themselves.

Best of all, Pat and Helen grew roses. In fact, roses were their passion. They experimented with different strains, and each year brought out unique colors and styles from that portion of their garden dedicated to rosebushes. Of course, with their generous spirits, they shared their roses with everyone. Those beauties appeared on neighbors' front porches, at the church, and in gift baskets that Pat and Helen took with them when they visited friends and relatives.

When our own daughters were born, Pat and Helen arrived soon after with a vase full of fresh roses from their garden. Roses represented life, beauty, and goodness. Together, they carefully cared for and pruned their rosebushes. Together, they smiled when they shared those roses with other people.

Years after we had moved away from their community, my wife and I went back to visit. Pat had recently died, and we had not seen Helen since his death. We looked forward to greeting her and checking in on how life had been progressing now that she was living alone.

Early in the evening, we stopped into the church to take a look around. To our surprise, Helen was there, and she was placing roses in the church. A beautiful arrangement of her finest flowers—red, white, pink, and the extraordinarily lovely Double Delight. Simply gorgeous.

Needless to say, we were thrilled to see Helen and delighted to see again the fruits of her gardening skills. I hugged her and said, "Your roses are so beautiful. It is so good to see you and your flowers again."

She fussed over the flowers a bit, paused, and then said, "Do you think so? I just didn't know if the roses would bloom without Pat."

Helen found it difficult to imagine gardening without her husband. He was a part of her, and she a part of him. She really could not see where she ended and Pat began. Two lives, so merged that it was almost impossible to conceive of one living without the other. And the roses embodied that.

Have you ever seen a joyful miser? Probably not.

_____

Money

9.1

9.2

9.3

9.4

9.5

What You Bring

Talk to any divorce attorney and they will likely tell you the same thing: The subject they hear about most often from their clients is money.

Disputes over money can erode a marriage quicker than arguments about any other topic. So it's important here and now to get clear about money and your family. Honest conversations now can help prevent an expectations gap later. You want to prevent the disappointment, resentment, anger, frustration, and loss of trust that can occur when the two of you hold different expectations about your finances.

How do you prevent that expectations gap? By discussing money, how you and your family viewed it and used it, and how you hope to use money in your life together.

Remember, everyone thinks how they grew up is normal. Like in Session 8, we assume that the way life was for us was the same for most of the people around us.

It's true for family, and it's also true for money. We tend to associate with people who have about the same amount of money we do. We tend to live around people who have about the same amount of money we do. That leads us to assume that most people have the same habits with money that our family does. However, we rarely know the real financial situations and habits of the people around us.

It's important here and now to get clear about money and your family.

Remember again from Session 8: we tend to re-create what we know from our families of origin. In the same way, we often re-create the same kind of spending, saving, and giving habits that we learned growing up.

Now the two of you get to decide what kind of family you want to be and create it. You also get to decide together what will be the financial priorities and habits in your relationship. What role do you want money to play in your family?

> My father and mother worked very hard. They both loved their work, but they did not make a lot of money. We lived very simply. My father handled the finances in our family. He was a saver. Very careful with money. No fancy vacations, no luxuries, nothing like that. But we always had what we needed. If my brother and I wanted something extra, we learned early on that we would need to earn the money to pay for it ourselves. I think that was good for us. We learned to work hard too.
>
> As a result, I think I have learned some of my father's habits. I rarely spend money on anything I would consider extravagant. Expensive things make me uncomfortable. And I like to save, so that I know I have a cushion just in case something happens.

Everyone thinks how they grew up is normal. And it is normal. . . for you. That's why the first step toward unity and purpose with money is to listen to where your partner comes from in this area.

So think about these questions. What was your experience with money growing up? What were your family's habits around giving, spending, and saving money? And what is your experience with money personally up until now?

Exercise:

Share your own family money story with your mate.

- What was your family like? Who paid the bills?
- What did your family tend to spend money on?
- Did your family like to save?
- Did your family like to give?
- Did your family use credit cards?
- What was financially important in your family? What was never important?
- When it came to money, what was your father like? Your mother? Your siblings?
- Describe your experience with money with your family and up until now. What financial habits do you have?
- What concerns you most about money?

....
....
....
....
....
....
....
....
....
....
....
....
....
....
....
....
....
....

All the wealth in the world cannot be compared with the happiness of living together happily united.

—**Blessed Marguerite d'Youville**

Reflect:

- What were a few things that surprised you about your spouse's family and money stories?
- What new things did you learn?

....

....

....

....

....

....

....

....

....

....

....

....

....

....

....

....

....

....

....

....

....

....

....

....

....

....

....

....

....

....

Notes

Money

9.1

9.2

9.3

9.4

9.5

Your Money Dream

There is nothing more powerful than sharing a dream as a couple and then pursuing that dream together. Now that you know each other's money stories, let's dream about what you want your financial story to be as your own family.

God has a dream for money. Very simply, he wants you to use money and love people—and never to get that backward. Too often we reverse that principle, and we love money and use people. But money is a tool to achieve goals. It is never the goal.

God made money so you can use it to love him and to love people. It's that simple. Use money for good—for your needs and the needs of others. Loving money is never an option. In fact, Scripture teaches us that the love of money is the root of all kinds of evil. Money is good only as a tool to love God and to love people.

Loving money is such a strong temptation for us that Jesus spent more time talking about money than he did any other topic. More time talking about money than He did talking about heaven, hell, sex or marriage. Because we humans love stuff. And when you love money and stuff, before long your stuff owns you more than you own it.

In the end, we can serve only one master. That's why Jesus famously said, "No servant can serve two masters; for either he will hate the one and love the other, or he will be devoted to the one and despise the other. You cannot serve God and mammon" (Luke 16:13).

Mammon is money and stuff—wealth. Jesus is clear: You cannot serve God and wealth. No one can serve two masters.

Think about it: Would you rather be in a relationship with a generous person or a stingy person? Probably a generous person. Why? Because their generosity spills into everything about them. They like to share. They care about others. They help when someone is in need. Generosity, kindness, and compassion. Those are all virtues we want in our relationships and in ourselves.

No one can serve two masters.

Would you rather be in a relationship with someone who wastes money frivolously or with someone who saves and prepares for a rainy day? The latter, probably. Why? Because preparation for hard times gives our lives some sense of stability and security. We all want that.

So as you think about your family, as you dream about your financial life, consider it from the positive perspective first. What are some things or qualities that you definitely want in your family when it comes to money? Perhaps you want a family in which you own your own home. Perhaps you want to be sure that you are the spouse who handles the money; perhaps not. Or you might desire to be a family that gives to the Church or to help people in need. Maybe you want to be able to afford to have only one of you working full-time so the other can be full-time with your children. Or you might hope to pray together regularly about financial decisions.

Then dream about your family's finances from the opposite perspective. What are some things or qualities that you definitely do not want in your family when it comes to money? Sometimes we are clearer about that than we are about what we do want. For example, my wife knew for sure that she did not want to manage our finances. She loathes that area of life and it was important to her not to have primary responsibility for it. Or maybe you want a home where no one argues about money and how it is spent. Or perhaps you definitely do not want to own your own home because of the pressure that goes with that. What are some financial things that you definitely do not want?

Discuss:

What are some financial things or qualities that you definitely want in your family? What are some financial things or qualities that you definitely do not want in your family?

A person's rightful
due is to be treated as
an object of love, not
as an object for use.

—St. John Paul II

Money

9.1

9.2

9.3

9.4

9.5

Saving

Storms are coming. Rainy days will arrive. The question is not *if* they will happen, but when.

This is true for various parts of your family and marriage, and it is especially true when it comes to money. Your wife's job might be eliminated. Your husband may be diagnosed with an illness that limits his ability to work and substantially increases your cost of living. Your parents might need assistance as they age, or your children may have special needs that require financial commitment on your family's part. You cannot predict what financial surprises, even storms, will come your way. But you can know they will come.

When my friend Clark went off to college, he returned home for Thanksgiving his first year. His father looked ashen, as if he were terminally ill and near death. Clark worried that his father might be dying from cancer and not have told him. When Thanksgiving dinner ended, his father called Clark into a private room in their house and confided in him. "Son, I have lost everything. My business has failed. We have nothing to support you. We can't afford for you to go back to college."

Prepare for

the storms

Clark was thrilled. He'd thought his father was dying when he only had suffered bankruptcy. Clark discovered that he needed to plan to support himself from that point on. Most important, he also learned to prepare for the storm. Seeing his father in such anguish stirred in Clark a resolve to never be caught without a backup plan or safety net in his own life. Save now so that you will be prepared later.

The Scriptures teach us a lot about preparation:

> *A wise man plans ahead; a fool doesn't and even brags about it!* (Proverbs 13:16)

> *The wise store up choice food and olive oil, but fools gulp theirs down.* (Proverbs 21:20)

The point is obvious: Some will be prepared; some will not. Be one of the prepared ones.

Saving 10 percent of your income from the very first day you are married is a marvelous goal. Perhaps you can start that immediately, or it may take you a year or two to get there. Set a saving goal for the year in January and then have monthly conversations about how you are doing in achieving that goal. Prepare for the storms. Make ready for the rainy day.

Life is choices. Being willing to delay gratification now in order to save for a better future will pay off in ways you can never imagine. But we live in a microwave culture. Slow cookers are frowned on. We want our French fries and we want them now! However, slow, steady saving and preparing has real value—everyday tangible value. Peace-of-mind value.

If you saved $1 a day for 55 years you would have $20,000 in savings. You may say, So what? Well, if you invested your $30 at the end of each month in government bonds at a return of 5 percent, after 55 years you would have $101,000. Still not convinced that you should delay your gratification? Invest your $1 a day at a return of 9 percent and after 55 years you will have $481,795.

Still not convinced? Save an entire $3 a day for 55 years and invest it at 9 percent and you will walk away with $1,445,385. That's right, almost $1.5 million in return for $3 a day of delayed gratification. Now, that would provide some peace of mind for you, would it not?

How valuable the peace of mind that comes from knowing you are prepared for a storm when it arrives. Your family may never need it, but they will thank you for the security and stability they experienced. That peace of mind is far more valuable than a big-screen TV will ever be.

Pray Together:

Lord Jesus, teach me to be generous;
Teach me to serve you as you deserve,
To give and not to count the cost,
To fight and not to heed the wounds,
To toil and not to seek for rest,
To labor and not to seek reward,
Except that of knowing that I do your will.

Amen.

—St. Ignatius of Loyola

Money

9.1

9.2

9.3

9.4

9.5

Giving

It sounds backward, but it isn't. **Your heart follows your money.**

"For where your treasure is, there your heart will be also"
(Matthew 6:21).

Your heart follows your money, and we usually think it is the other way around. We think that we fall in love with something and then our money follows it. But the opposite is true. If you want to see what your heart is attached to, take a look at where you spend your money.

When I was in high school, I discovered girls and quickly decided I wanted to spend more time with them. That meant I needed a car. But I had no money. So I went to my father and asked him to buy me a car so I could go out with girls. He laughed. In my face.

So I got a part-time job, working after school at a sporting goods store selling tennis shoes and socks and that kind of stuff. I saved my money and I saved. To buy that car.

I found an old Volkswagen, beat up, rusty, and ugly. But it ran and I could afford it. So I spent every dollar I had on that car, just so I could go out with girls.

It wasn't a great car, to be honest. It had no air conditioning. It made a lot of noise when it ran. And it had holes in it. Anytime it rained the rear passenger floorboard filled up with water. Which was kind of cool. Because when a girl was riding in the front passenger side and we stopped at a red light, that water would slide up under the seat and wash her feet. And then when I started up again at the green light, the water would recede into the rear floorboard again and the girl's feet could dry. It was the only car at my high school with a foot-washing device. Very cool.

But you know what happened after I bought that car? Every Saturday, I would get up early, wash it, wax it, Armor All the dashboard and the tires, and Windex the windshield. I spent hours every Saturday morning just taking care of it. I could not spend enough time with it. I loved that car. Why? Because every single penny I had ever made was spent on it. I was attached to it.

Your heart follows your money.

Why does this matter? Because Jesus wants your heart. And if you're not careful, your heart gets attached to stuff; it gets attached to where your money is. Jesus knows that the greatest competitor he has for your heart is your money, your stuff.

How do we remedy that problem of our hearts being attached to stuff? With generous giving.

Giving frees my heart from the idea that it all belongs to me, when in fact it all belongs to God.

Generosity liberates us to care about other people as much as we care about ourselves.

Generous giving helps us detach from stuff and attach to God.

Again, think about it. Who would you rather be in a relationship with: a generous person or a stingy person?

A generous person, right? Because we all like being around people who are generous, who care about other people, who aren't stingy and cheap. Have you ever been around someone who is always keeping score about every penny and every dollar either of you spends? Always wanting to look for the cheapest option even when you know it won't be any good? That person usually sucks the joy out of every situation.

Generosity gives life. Stinginess sucks life. Generosity leads to joy. Stinginess leads to misery, which is where we get the word miser. Have you ever seen a joyful miser? Probably not.

Jesus wants your heart. And when you give it to him in your generosity, you discover the joy of selflessness, the joy of compassion, and the joy of mission.

Exercise:

Set a giving goal together. 10 percent is a wonderful goal. If that seems out of reach, take a look at what percentage of your income you presently give to ministries and charities and to help others. Add 1 percentage point to that this year and begin to grow from there. For example, if you gave away 1.5 percent last year, make your goal to give 2.5 percent this year. And then grow by one percentage point each year until you reach 10 percent.

OR

Dream together about a ministry or charity you hope to support and help throughout your marriage. Set a goal of an amount or a percentage of your income that you eventually hope to be able to give to that ministry. Then begin with a first step now, whether it is ten, a hundred, or a thousand dollars a month, as you move toward that dream together.

The things that we
love tell us what
we are.

—St. Thomas Aquinas

Money

9.1

9.2

9.3

9.4

9.5

Your Money Fears

What are your biggest fears around money? Be honest.

Very few subjects make us more nervous than money. So be honest; it will serve your marriage well.

Maybe you have a lot of credit card debt and you fear that you will never get back to a zero balance. You may fear going bankrupt someday and experiencing that financial distress. Possibly your greatest fear is not being able to afford your children's education or not being able to retire because you don't have enough money. You might be afraid of feeling the anxiety and worry that goes with always being behind in your finances. What is your biggest financial fear? The only way to address it is to know what you are afraid of and develop a plan to face it together.

It is important to know that this area of money, love, and marriage is where the BETTER TOGETHER lessons on dreams and conflict resolution will most often play out in your real life as a couple.

Remember the divorce attorney question: What is the topic you hear about the most often from your clients seeking divorce? If the attorney is honest, he or she will respond, "The number one source of conflict I hear about is money." Financial disagreements are not necessarily the main cause of divorce, but they are usually a major contributor.

Financial instability destroys families. Lack of a clear financial plan creates constant stress and produces a baseline anxiety, worry, and fear that spill into all the other areas of your life together.

The antidote to that anxiety is stability. And the road to stability runs through a budget—one that you discuss, draft, and agree on together.

When you were single, you were lord and master of your budget. You may not have even had one.

Who, being loved,
is poor?

—Oscar Wilde

Now that you are married, there will naturally be two voices speaking into how you use money, how you earn, spend, save, and give it. Your financial life will now be more of a negotiation than a one-sided decision.

There are good and bad ways to approach negotiation, especially when you are negotiating on a delicate subject (money) with someone you love deeply (your spouse). Healthy discussions will make each of you feel safe. You will listen as much as you talk. You will give up the idea of single-handedly maintaining full control of all things financial.

Compromise lies at the very center of negotiation. Not everyone can have everything they want. That is true for every family, whether making ten thousand or ten million dollars a year. We are in this together. We will each embody what it means to give and take.

Because in the end, love is not about compromise. Love is about sacrifice.

When you are willing to give up something (or part of something) to help make the whole thing work, then you are loving well. And when you are both willing to give up something to make your dream together a reality, that sacrifice loves most of all.

Love is patient and kind; love is not jealous or boastful; it is not arrogant or rude. Love does not insist on its own way; it is not irritable or resentful; it does not rejoice at wrong, but rejoices in the right.

(1 Corinthians 13:4-6)

Exercise:

Draft a simple budget together.

MONTHLY BUDGET

Monthly Bills		% Income	Paid	Income
Mortgage/ Rent			☐	
Insurance			☐	
Car Insurance			☐	
Gas Bill			☐	
Electric Bill			☐	
Sewer Bill			☐	
Water Bill			☐	
Student Loans			☐	
Cell Phone			☐	
Internet			☐	
Church Donations			☐	
Charitable Donations			☐	
TV			☐	
Streaming Services			☐	
			☐	
			☐	
			☐	
			☐	Income Per Month
			☐	— Total Monthly Bills

Total Monthly Bills: **Total Spendable Income:**

Expenses		% Income		
Savings				
Grocery				
Gas				
Fun				
				Total Spendable Income
				— Total Expenses

Total Expenses: **Over/Under Budget:**

How One Couple Uses a Budget to Navigate Life and Avoid Financial Fears

Every year, in January, Christian and Carla sit down to dream about the future of their life and their marriage. They sit across from each other at a coffee shop, break out their laptops, and dream about what the next year could look like. The focus quickly turns to how to make those dreams a reality, and the purpose of this annual meeting is to plan how to achieve those dreams financially.

They call it the annual board meeting. They take stock of the dreams they've achieved, update on the dreams they are still working toward, examine what has gone wrong, and decide how they can best use their finances in the next year.

Then, each month, they have a brief follow-up meeting. One night after dinner, they look over the monthly budget. They track spending, Christian lovingly teasing Carla about her unusually large coffee budget and Carla giving Christian a hard time about splurging on a new piece of music equipment—but it's all done in good fun. They plan for the month ahead, update their progress on their annual financial goals, and always make sure they plan out some fun for the next month.

The budget meetings and the annual board meeting are one of Christian and Carla's favorite parts about being married. They look forward to their meetings each month. Their finances, which are usually a source of stress and constraint in a marriage, have become something that actually opens communication and brings them closer.

Notes

Additional Resources

What the Church, the Bible, and the Saints Teach
Us About the Sacrament of Marriage

Daily Giving

St. Paul teaches that marriage is a sacrament of the covenant Christ has with his people. This is true because spouses pledge to each other all aspects of their lives "until death do us part." Just as Christ gave his entire life for the Church, he invites us to give our whole selves to him in return. A marriage mirrors that same complete, unconditional giving to each other.

Total fidelity in your marriage does not just mean that you stay married. It requires daily action, and it requires intentionality. Are you going to work at and invest in this marriage? Will you be faithful physically, emotionally, spiritually, and intellectually? Will you commit to helping each other become the-best-version-of-yourselves?

In daily acts of kindness, mutual love, and forgiveness, couples imitate, however imperfectly, the unconditional love Christ offers us. Those small daily acts root a marriage in the covenant of love between God and humanity.

CATECHISM

1609 In his mercy God has not forsaken sinful man. The punishments consequent upon sin, "pain in child-bearing" and toil "in the sweat of your brow," also embody remedies that limit the damaging effects of sin. After the fall, marriage helps to overcome self-absorption, egoism, pursuit of one's own pleasure, and to open oneself to the other, to mutual aid and to self-giving.

2365 Fidelity expresses constancy in keeping one's given word. God is faithful. The Sacrament of Matrimony enables man and woman to enter into Christ's fidelity for his Church. Through conjugal chastity, they bear witness to this mystery before the world.

St. John Chrysostom suggests that young husbands should say to their wives: I have taken you in my arms, and I love you, and I prefer you to my life itself. For the present life is nothing, and my most ardent dream is to spend it with you in such a way that we may be assured of not being separated in the life reserved for us. . . I place your love above all things, and nothing would be more bitter or painful to me than to be of a different mind than you.

SCRIPTURE

Finally, brothers, whatever is true, whatever is honorable, whatever is just, whatever is pure, whatever is lovely, whatever is gracious, if there is any excellence and if there is anything worthy of praise, think about these things. (Philippians 4:8)

"The only way I can prove my love is by scattering flowers, and these flowers are every little sacrifice, every glance and word, and the doing of the least actions for love."

St. Thérèse de Lisieux has taught us that our souls become greater or lesser based on the little things we choose to do each day. It is true for your soul and it is true for your marriage.

_____

Generosity gives life.

The Most
Important
in a Marri

A successful marriage requires
falling in love many times, always
with the same person.

—**Mignon McLaughlin**

The Most
Important Word
in a Marriage

SESSION 10

Wisdom for Forgiveness from Mitch

———————

Mitch never saw it coming. Not at all. It just never occurred to him.

At Dynamic Catholic's Passion and Purpose for Marriage events, we focus on providing helpful and inspiring ways for couples to reenergize their relationships. I enjoy these half-day events because they are filled as much with laughter as with serious moments.

As part of that experience, couples are invited to do a simple fill-in-the-blank exercise.

It goes something like this: The man and woman sit, hold hands, and face each other. The woman goes first, and I invite her to say, "Please forgive me for _____." She should fill in the blank with something simple for which she desires her husband's forgiveness. I instruct him to respond with only these three words: "I forgive you." No more, no less.

Then the spouses switch roles, and the husband fills in the same blank and asks his wife for forgiveness. Again, she responds with just those three words: "I forgive you."

Two days after leading one of these events, I received a phone call from an attendee, Mitch. He called our office and insisted on talking to me. Frankly, I assumed he wanted to complain about something. On the contrary, he eagerly wanted to share what had happened during that simple fill-in-the-blank exchange with his wife. He had assumed this exchange might be helpful for other couples but certainly not for him and his wife.

"I couldn't believe it," he said. "I thought I knew what was going to happen. My wife was going to say something kind of generic that she wanted me to forgive. Next, I'd give her a basic forgiveness like you said, and then we'd switch. But instead, she sat there for a long time in silence. I started getting nervous. Still more silence. Finally she said, 'Please forgive me for being bitter.'"

Over the phone, Mitch's voice got very serious.

"I was taken aback. I had no idea what she was talking about. I didn't know what to say or do, so I said, 'What do you mean? Bitter? About what?'

"My wife continued, 'Two years ago, when we had that fight. Do you remember?'"

Mitch shook his head tentatively, not really recalling what she was describing.

"You know. That night you got up and stormed out of the bedroom. You went downstairs and slept in the guest room in the basement."

A light went on in Mitch's head. He remembered the argument. When he had gotten up out of bed, he had screamed at her, "That's it! I've had enough. I just can't take this life anymore." She said, "Ever since then, I've wondered if you were going to leave us. I've been anxious. I've been scared that the next fight would be our last. And I've become bitter. Please forgive me." What Mitch thought had been just a one-time moment of frustration had instead been something completely different for his wife. For her, that argument had been a life-changing conversation. He had not given that fight a second thought, while she had been continually reliving it for two years.

Mitch never saw her honesty coming. He thought there was nothing between them at all. Instead, she spoke the truth and revealed the wall of bitterness that had slowly grown to separate them over those two years. What Mitch had seen as a small, almost insignificant thing was actually huge in his wife's eyes and in their marriage.

At that moment, God removed the scales that had prevented Mitch from clearly seeing his wife and her deep hurts. His eyes opened. His heart softened. And he knew what needed to happen next.

He quickly forgave her bitterness. And then he promptly apologized for having created it in the first place with his harsh words and cold demeanor.

Forgiveness given; forgiveness received. Mitch had called our office to say thank you because he had never seen it coming, but he was sure glad it had. True wisdom.

The Most Important
Word in a Marriage

_____

Nuclear Power

Marriage is deeply intimate. And marriage is every day. That combination of deep intimacy every day gives marriage tremendous power.

Some relationships are intimate, like your relationship with your mother, or your brother, or maybe even a very close friend. You know each other's deepest secrets. You become very familiar with each other's good habits and bad habits. You can be your true self in an intimate relationship. And you get a glimpse of the other person's true self as well.

In marriage, that is especially true. You share the same bed. You probably share the same bathroom and the same kitchen. You wake up and see each other first thing in the morning in all your unmade-up glory. You share bank accounts and resources. You may share children. You smell each other. You hear each other. And hopefully you deeply listen to each other. Marriage is supremely intimate.

And some of your relationships are with people you see almost every day, like a coworker or a roommate. But marriage brings a whole new level to the term everydayness. It is every single day. You live in the same space each day. Always. You see each other at your best and at your worst, every day. And when you have children, they are there every day—and often awake every night.

Unlike other relationships, only marriage combines those two aspects: deeply intimate and every day. And that combination gives marriage a power unlike any other—an almost nuclear power.

Your marriage has incredible power to build you up. To help each of you become the-best-version-of-yourselves. To give you life. To encourage you to grow in virtues like love, patience, and kindness. It can help you get to heaven.

But marriage, because of that intimacy and everydayness, also has the tremendous power to harm, to hurt, or to injure. In toxic marriages, one partner can inflict damage on the other in remarkable ways. Sometimes, a toxic marriage can even destroy.

There are more than seven billion people on planet earth. Each of us is wonderfully made in the image of God. Each of us is also imperfect. So there are seven billion wonderful, imperfect people on this planet. You and your spouse are two of them. Each of you possesses some beautiful, endearing strengths. Those strengths will give life to your marriage and your family. And each of you also has some weaknesses, some areas for growth. Those areas probably frustrate you at times, and they will frustrate your spouse and family. In other words, both you and your spouse are fully human.

Because you are two wonderful, imperfect humans, living together every day in an intimate way, you will need to learn how to live together in the most life-giving way. And that will take work, real on-the-job training. Day by day, year by year, the two of you will discover how to build each other up, how to tolerate and laugh at your imperfections, and how to prosper. In other words, you will find your own way to be better together.

Marriage has power. And if that is the case, we need to figure out how to harness that nuclear power for the greatest good of all.

Your marriage has incredible power to build you up.

Pray Together:

Lord
Open my eyes
And see the amazing world You
    have created
In the hundreds of thousands of
    stars
You have found a place for me

You have blessed my life
With wisdom
With imagination
With spirit

You constantly write love letters
    to me
In Your creation
Your fingerprints upon every
    particle

Each drop of rain contains Your
    world
What colour the kingfisher
    carries
The wildflowers bow in the
    breeze
All tides and seas
Know the song of Your creation

Evening light that fades
Bringing night in dewy haze
Your gift O God
Our time of contemplation

Lord
May we mirror Your beauty
For we are made of You
We complete Your universe

May all we do
May all we think
Be a song of joy

May we add our voices
To the song of monks
In the quiet hours of night
Who wait patiently for the dawn

May we never grow weary
Of mystery
Of beauty
Of searching
For restless is the heart
Until we find our home in You
And with You
And with ourselves

For in You we move
And have Your being
Yet no ear has heard
Nor eye has seen
What You have prepared
For those
Who want to love
You.

—Fr. Liam Lawton,
    from *The Hope Prayer*

The Most Important
Word in a Marriage

Imperfect and Selfish

You and your betrothed are wonderful and imperfect.

Because your husband is imperfect, he will at times say or do things that disappoint or hurt you. Because your wife is imperfect, she will at times forget to say or do things that you would like her to say or do. When this happens, she will disappoint or hurt you. This is what humans do. We can often be selfish creatures, and we can be thoughtless.

- We fail to remember an anniversary or a birthday.
- We say something thoughtless or unkind about our in-laws.
- We forget to go to the grocery store when we said we would.
- We don't help the children with their homework when we promised to.
- We do not love as generously as we hope to.
- We bring up an old relationship in a petty way in the heat of an argument.

We slip. We fall. We're human beings. We are wonderful and we are imperfect.

Life is choices. And when your spouse hurts your feelings or disappoints your expectations or fails to recognize your needs, you have a choice in how you respond. Really, you have three choices.

You can:

1. **Retaliate.** You can choose to be an emotional boomerang. When your spouse injures you, you can exact revenge and hurt him or her back. Humans frequently like to do this. You hurt me, then I will hurt you. Quid pro quo. Tit for tat. I'll let you know just how hurt you made me feel by making you feel that pain too.

2. **Resent.** You can choose to hold your hurt and disappointment inside and let it simmer and stew. You can't respond when your spouse wounds you, so instead you place that

wound in your inner slow cooker and just let it sit there for weeks, even years. You might add to it with other wounds over the years, until one day your inner slow cooker explodes and you spread all those pent-up wounds and injuries in one huge disastrous moment. You are a human being, and you might choose the path of resentment.

3. **Release.** You can choose a third way: the path of forgiveness, and her cousin grace. Grace does not ignore the hurt or the wound. Grace is no doormat. Grace acknowledges the injury, but it absorbs the hurt, and then releases it. Forgiveness and grace are supernatural. Rather than retaliating or resenting, forgiveness absorbs and releases so that the relationship can move forward. The poison has been removed.

Forgiveness unleashes a power unlike any other in the universe. Forgiveness transforms. It transforms people. It transforms relationships. It transforms families. It can transform the world. Marriage has tremendous power, but forgiveness is the most powerful word in the English language. And it certainly is the most powerful word in your marriage.

Forgiveness releases the pain and offers a second chance. Forgiveness brings redemption, then growth in the relationship. Forgiveness believes that we humans not only can change and become better-versions-of-ourselves, but that we will frequently do so when given the chance. Forgiveness refuses to let the past rob you of your future together.

When you choose forgiveness and grace, you are giving your spouse the benefit of the doubt. You are reminding yourself and your spouse that you know your spouse loves you, and that they want what's best for you and for the marriage. They may have just said or done something that could harm the marriage or breed resentment, but you are giving them the benefit of the doubt and pointing to a way forward. You love them and want what's best for your mate and what's best for your marriage and future.

More important, when you choose forgiveness and grace, you are recognizing that your spouse is imperfect. And you are not giving in to the temptation to hold her or him to the impossible standard of perfection. You are also recognizing that you yourself are imperfect and placing hope that your spouse will also not hold you to a standard that you cannot meet. You give forgiveness and grace because you know that soon you will need it in return.

You and your spouse are wonderful and imperfect, so forgiveness and grace will be your best friends. Best of all, forgiveness will transform each of you and the marriage itself. Because it is the most powerful word in the universe.

Reflect:

What is God saying to you in this section?

There is no place for selfishness—and no place for fear! Do not be afraid, then, when love makes demands. Do not be afraid when love requires sacrifice.

—St. John Paul II

The Most Important Word in a Marriage

It's Who We Are

If anyone should understand and embrace forgiveness, it's us: Catholics. We're different. When it comes to forgiveness, we have an entire office for it: **the sacrament of Reconciliation**. It's an opportunity to experience the grace and forgiveness of Christ every time we enter and open ourselves to the priest and the merciful power of the divine.

Forgiveness is who we are. It's not merely something we do. We are the people of forgiveness.

Think about Jesus, who is teaching his disciples one day when Peter says, "Lord, if one of my brothers injures me, how many times do I have to forgive him? Seven?" You can almost feel Peter blow up with pride and confidence. Seven is a big number. It's hard to forgive someone seven times for the same thing. So Peter thinks he is offering a huge, bold new way forward. Forgiving someone seven times.

Have you ever forgiven someone for the same thing seven times? Well, you will soon. You're getting married!

But remember Jesus' response to Peter: "No, not seven times. But seven times seventy times." Four hundred and ninety? Wow. Jesus takes Peter's boldness and expands it exponentially! Jesus is radical about forgiveness.

Jesus is so radical about forgiveness that we see it most of all on the day of his death. Remember how they crucified him. They placed his body on the cross, flat on the ground, nailed him to it, and then lifted it up to place it erect, in a hole in the ground. That likely was the most painful moment for Jesus, when the cross stood erect and all the force of gravity pulled his body toward the earth in one massive jolt. But his body remained suspended, resisting gravity only by the strength of those nails through his hands.

Jesus hung there for hours. His body drooping. The sun beating down on him, dehydrating him. The crowd mocking him. He occasionally would have had to pull himself up to try to breathe in some oxygen. To pull up, he would have had to use the little bit of strength remaining in his body to push himself up on the nails in his feet and pull up through the nails in his hands. The pain must have been excruciating.

And as he hung there, soldiers stood guard beneath the cross. They noticed Jesus' seamless garment lying there on the ground nearby. Seamless garments were valuable, so the soldiers began to quibble over which of them might take home that garment after his death. Soon, they decided to cast lots to decide who would get the seamless garment of Jesus.

Jesus hung there, dying, watching the soldiers argue for his clothing below. He looked down, and rather than choosing to rain down anger and wrath on them, he pulled himself up one more time. In one of his last breaths on earth, one of his final moments in life, Jesus looked into the face of God the Father and said, "Father, forgive them. They don't know what they're doing."

Jesus forgives. Even until the end.

We almost take Jesus and forgiveness for granted, as if forgiveness were not as radical as it was and is. The forgiveness of Christ is a huge break from the religious tradition that still dominates much of the world today: an eye for an eye. Jesus broke from the path of retaliation. He ended the cycle of perpetual revenge. Instead of death, he offered new life and redemption.

We follow Jesus. Forgiveness is not something we do as Catholics. It is who we are.

Marriage has great power. But forgiveness harnesses the greatest power of all. It changes lives, changes relationships, changes families, and changes the world.

Reflect:

Think of a time when you forgave your future spouse. Now remember a time when he or she forgave you.

Pray Together:

AN ACT OF HOPE

When faith falters,
Virtue fails,
And deeds of love are few,
Then, Lord, I pray
That we may turn in hope to you.
So why are we disheartened
When those whom we appoint
Reveal themselves as only human
And inevitably disappoint?
May we hope not in our strength,
Wisdom, goodness, nor our reason,
Not in our economy, technology,
Nor the latest, greatest of a season.
Turn our eyes to you, Beloved One,
Beauty, ever ancient, ever new,
Birthing hope, not of our own making
But from you, in you, through you.
Jesus, I trust your words of hope,
Cutting deeper than a knife:
"I've come in love for only this—
That you may have New Life!"

—Fr. J. Michael Sparough, SJ
Beautiful Hope

The Most Important Word in a Marriage

The Way

Millie had made an awful mistake, and she wanted to come home. She desired no more, and she could accept no less.

Married at age eighteen, Millie grew restless ten years later. With three kids to care for, and all the weight of adulthood bearing down on her shoulders, she soon found excitement in the arms of another man. For four months, she met this man clandestinely, and their passionate love affair gripped her entire life.

After four months of meeting her lover in motels and parked cars, Millie left her husband, Tom, and three children. She moved in with her paramour. They set up house in the same town, just a few miles away from her husband and kids. Tom was devastated, but he refused to give up on her, their vows, and their family. He wrote her notes. He left her messages. On one occasion, he physically picked her up and took her to church to meet with their pastor. But Millie rejected all of his efforts, even going as far as telling the pastor, "I don't need you. I don't want this. I am finished with all of you."

For nearly a year, Millie reveled in her newfound freedom. No kids. No responsibilities. Just the passion and thrill of being in love with someone new. Or so she thought.

The whole time, her husband had made it known that he was waiting for her. Tom left messages. He left notes reading, "I'm not giving up on us. This is not where you belong and this is not who you are."

On a Wednesday morning, Millie woke up, in more ways than one. That morning, reality sank in. Her mind focused, and she thought, "What in the world have I done?" She knew she was making the biggest mistake of her life. All the decisions of the past year collapsed around her. She had taken a man who loved her unconditionally, and the children they had created together, and ditched that on the side of the road like a used cigarette butt. The crushing wave of what she had chosen washed over her. And she decided, "I am going home."

Millie had no expectation that her husband would forgive her. She hoped he would at least welcome her. She merely wanted to come home. That was all. To be back in the place where she belonged. Whether she could set things right or not did not matter, because at least she would be home.

Millie pulled into the driveway and went to the front door. She heard the kids playing in the backyard and stood there on the doorstep for a very long time. It was Wednesday night, right before her husband and children would leave to attend church. After what felt like a decade, Millie knocked on the door. Tom opened the front door and she could not look up at him. She was shaking and ashamed.

Her husband took the first step. He placed his hands on Millie's face and held her chin up. Looking into her face, Tom said, "Welcome home."

She responded, "I wanna come home."

And he pulled her small body to him, and that was it.

They prayed. Millie cried. Tom cried.

A week later, Millie discovered that she was pregnant. The news meant one obvious thing: She was carrying the child of her lover. Millie was broken. Adultery. Illegitimate child. Husband. Three children depending on her. The gravity of her mistake crushed her. One week home, one week of moving toward making things right, and now this. An unexpected and fully unwanted pregnancy with a child who could be a permanent reminder of the biggest mistake Millie had ever made and the very real and deep pain she had inflicted on her family. She knew what she wanted to do: end the pregnancy.

That evening, Millie broke the news to her husband. Like he had done on the doorstep of their home a week before, Tom looked her in the eye and said, "This is going to be all right." Millie shared that she did not believe that she could go through with the pregnancy. The pain of the living reminder of her adultery was simply too great to bear. He told her that they would make something wonderful from the pain and raise the baby together.

Fortunately, the paramour did not want anything to do with the child, and Millie and Tom now have another lovely daughter. Her in-laws and closest friends, the handful of people who knew the complete story, welcomed the baby just as they had welcomed Millie home upon her return.

Some of the people in town know, and they ask Tom, "How could you have taken her back? How could you have forgiven her?" He replies the same way each time: "You know, with all that Christ did to forgive me, how could I look at my wife, the woman he gave me to love, and say, 'You know, you've done something so horrible that I can't forgive you'?"

Her husband's generous forgiveness brought Millie home again, this time to stay. **His forgiveness brought a baby from death to life, a mother back to her children, his soul mate back to him, and a future to everyone involved.** Through forgiveness, Tom created a future of memories that will include grandchildren not yet born and mountaintops not yet reached.

All human nature vigorously resists grace because grace changes us and change is painful.

—Flannery O'Connor

Nelson Mandela taught the world about the power of grace. After he emerged from twenty-seven years in prison and was elected the new president of South Africa, his first act was to invite his jailer to join him on the presidential inauguration platform. Mandela then appointed Archbishop Desmond Tutu to head an official government panel with an intimidating name, the Truth and Reconciliation Commission (TRC), to try to bring the racially fractured nation together. Mandela wanted to defuse the natural human pattern of revenge that he had seen firsthand in prison and in so many countries where one race or tribe had taken control from another.

The TRC rules were simple: If a white policeman or army officer voluntarily faced his accusers, confessed his crime, and fully acknowledged his guilt, he could not be tried and punished for that crime. South African hard-liners grumbled about the injustice of letting criminals go free. Mandela, however, insisted that the country needed healing more than it needed justice.

Officer van de Broek certainly did not merit forgiveness. Anyone could see that. He had behaved like a depraved animal. Nevertheless, there he stood, and one woman had his fate in her hands, an unnamed South African woman, described by Philip Yancey in his Rumors of Another World.

At one hearing, Officer van de Broek, a policeman, shared how he and other officers had entered a village and shot an eighteen-year-old boy. After the murder, they burned the boy's body, turning it on the fire like a piece of barbecue meat in order to destroy the evidence. Eight years later, van de Broek returned to the same house and this time seized the boy's father. The man's wife was forced to watch as policemen bound her husband on a woodpile, poured gasoline over his body, and ignited it.

The courtroom grew hushed as the elderly woman who had lost first her son and then her husband listened to Officer van de Broek's confession. She was then given a chance to respond.

"What do you want from Mr. van de Broek?" the judge asked. The woman stood. She said she first wanted van de Broek to go to the place where they had burned her husband's body and gather up the dust so she could give him a decent burial. After all, that dust was all she had left of her family. His head down, the policeman nodded in agreement.

Then she added a second request. "Mr. van de Broek took all my family away from me, and I still have a lot of love to give," she said. "Twice a month, I would like for him to come to the ghetto and spend a day with me so I can be a mother to him. And I would like

Mr. van de Broek to know that he is forgiven by God, and that I forgive him too. I would like to embrace him so he can know my forgiveness is real."

Spontaneously, some of the observers who were gathered in the courtroom began singing "Amazing Grace" as the elderly woman made her way to the witness stand. Officer van de Broek did not hear the words of the hymn. He had fainted, completely overwhelmed.

Because of her, everyone in that room, including the man who had crushed her family, was changed by grace.

Exercise:

At Dynamic Catholic's Passion and Purpose for Marriage events, we focus on providing helpful and inspiring ways for couples to re-energize their relationships. These half-day events are filled as much with laughter as with serious moments.

As part of that experience, couples are invited to do a simple fill-in-the-blank exercise. **Try this exercise together as a couple:**

The man and woman sit, hold hands, and face each other. The woman goes first, and I invite her to say, "Please forgive me for _____ _____ ." She should fill in the blank with something simple for which she desires her husband's forgiveness. I instruct him to respond with only these three words: "I forgive you." No more, no less.

Then the spouses switch roles, and the husband fills in the same blank and asks his wife for forgiveness. Again, she responds with just those three words: "I forgive you."

This is a simple act. It often triggers a larger conversation later on. But at the events this exercise teaches or reminds husband and wife how to forgive.

The Most Important
Word in a Marriage

Your Spouse Is
Not God

Maybe it's because we're Catholic and we have the sacrament of Reconciliation. Maybe it's because we love the feeling of confessing our sins to the priest and then having him wipe the slate clean and offer us the mercy of Jesus. Or maybe it's because of something else.

But many of us Catholics bring that same confessional attitude to forgiveness in our relationships. We confess and apologize to someone we have wronged or hurt. Then we expect them to magically wipe the slate clean. **Somehow we expect them to behave like God.**

Forgiveness, however, is usually a process as much as it is a moment. When you sin against someone, you often think about it, reflect on it, and make your way toward an apology over time. When you actually apologize, it is the culmination of the process for you. But for the person receiving the apology, the process has really just begun. Your apology concludes your process, but their process may just be beginning.

It is important to recognize that the person you have hurt or wronged may need some time to work through forgiving you. Expecting them to do that instantaneously is expecting them to be God. He or she is human. He is not God. She is wonderful and imperfect, just like you.

Human beings process things, some slower, some faster. And your spouse is a human being.

Remember the expectations gap early on in BETTER TOGETHER? And how we set ourselves up for failure when we have unrealistic expectations of our spouse, and no one can meet expectations they don't know about?

No one person can meet or fulfill all of your needs. That is an unrealistic expectation. Yet, many marriages struggle to survive because one or both partners live with the belief that their spouse can and should meet all their needs. Only God can do that.

And your spouse is not God.

Be careful not to look to your spouse to fulfill a role that rightly belongs to God. He can forgive and erase sins in a moment. For us humans, that process of forgiveness and wiping the slate clean can take time. When you believe your spouse is like God, you set your spouse up to fail. And you set yourself up for disappointment, resentment, anger, frustration, and loss of trust. Those fill the expectations gap we create.

You want to set up your spouse to thrive and succeed. After all, that is what it means to be better together.

_____

Be careful not to look to your spouse to fulfill a role that rightly belongs to God.

PRAYER OF FORGIVENESS

Lord
Help me to be humble
For I have wandered
Far from Your goodness and lived
  just for myself
Give me the courage to be
  self-effacing and honest

Forgive me for the times I have
  imprisoned myself
In selfishness
In greed
In envy
In arrogance
In anger
In despair
In mistrust

Forgive me for falling into
Self-pity
Self-doubt
Self-destruction
Self-containment

May these times of falling and failing
Lead me to a greater understanding
  of myself
And a new appreciation of Your infinite goodness and mercy

Unbind me
From the dark clouds that veil my
life in fear
From the allurement of empty promises
From self-satisfaction
From the paralysis of self-loathing

To be humble
Is to come close to You
Who desires nothing more only
To love us as You do

Heal the deepest places of hurt
So that nothing is hidden from You
And the gaze of Your gentle eyes

In my sorrow
May I listen to the words of those
Who seek forgiveness from me
May I accept the sincerity of their
  hearts
So they too will know Your healing
  mercy
Through my pardon

Lord
Forgive my blindness
In failing to see Your abundant
  blessings
Given daily from Your kindness

Forgive me Lord
And let my shame now end

Forgive me Lord
That I would live again.

—Fr. Liam Lawton, from *The Hope Prayer*

Additional Resources

What the Church, the Bible, and the Saints Teach
Us About the Sacrament of Marriage

Reconciliation

We are a people of forgiveness. Love is not really love if it is not complete, total, and definitive. That loving, forgiving identity spills over into every aspect of our lives as baptized followers of Christ. That is exactly what St. Paul describes in the following passage of Scripture from Colossians.

CHURCH TEACHING

And because these words involve such solemn obligations, it is most fitting that you rest the security of your wedded life upon the great principle of self-sacrifice.

And so you begin your married life by the voluntary and complete surrender of your individual lives in the interest of that deeper and wider life which you are to have in common.

Henceforth you will belong entirely to each other; you will be one in mind, one in heart, and one in affections.

And whatever sacrifices you may hereafter be required to make to preserve this mutual life, always make them generously.

Sacrifice is usually difficult and irksome. Only love can make it easy, and perfect love can make it a joy.

We are willing to give in proportion as we love.

And when love is perfect, the sacrifice is complete.
—Archbishop William O. Brady, "Instruction on the Day of Marriage"

SCRIPTURE

As God's chosen ones, holy and beloved, clothe yourselves with compassion, kindness, humility, meekness, and patience. Bear with one another and, if anyone has a complaint against another, forgive each other; just as the Lord has forgiven you, so you also must forgive. Above all, clothe yourselves with love, which binds everything together in perfect harmony. And let the peace of Christ rule in your hearts, to which indeed you were called in the one body. And be thankful. Let the word of Christ dwell in you richly; teach and admonish one another in all wisdom; and with gratitude in your hearts sing psalms, hymns, and spiritual songs to God. And whatever you do, in word or deed, do everything in the name of the Lord Jesus, giving thanks to God the Father through him.
(Colossians 3:12–17)

SAINT

God's purpose is to make the soul great.
—St. John of the Cross

Notes

Better Day

When you make the sacrifice in marriage, you're sacrificing not to each other but to unity in a relationship.

—Joseph Campbell

Better Every Day

SESSION 11

Wisdom for True Love from Richard and Mary

I am an avid reader of online news, magazines, and print or electronic books. It was in a magazine that I came across the story of Richard and Mary, a story filled with so much marriage wisdom that I re-read it regularly for inspiration and help.

Richard served as the president of a college for about two decades. He and his wife, Mary, both were known for their excellent teaching and leadership. They had friends around the globe and were the envy of many who saw the passion and purpose with which they lived.

While speaking at an event in Florida, Mary repeated the same story five minutes after she had just told it. Richard thought that mistake was odd. It had not happened before. Mary was just fifty-five years old.

Repeating herself in public began to happen every so often, but not often enough to worry much about. Until three years later, when Mary went to the hospital for a heart problem she was experiencing. The doctor shared jarring news: She was suffering from Alzheimer's. Thus began the slow erosion of Mary and her remarkable sparkle and gifts.

Mary continued to accept public-speaking and teaching engagements. She would repeat herself in some settings, forget where she was in others, and mismatch thoughts before crowds, only to return home humiliated at her inability to perform like she always had. Her Alzheimer's worsened, slowly, like a glacier creeping into the crevices of her brain and her soul.

Soon Richard was scared to leave Mary alone, so they traveled everywhere together. Everywhere they went, if he took his eye off her for a moment, she wandered off. Mary was slipping away, literally and figuratively.

Caregivers at their home quit. The task of caring for Mary simply became overwhelming.

Their travel together soon became too much for Richard to handle as well. One flight in Atlanta was delayed for two hours. As they waited in the airport, Mary asked the same questions over and over. Every five minutes or so, she would take a fast-paced walk up and down the enormous terminal for no apparent reason. Richard had to jog to keep up with her. After one of those countless walks, a female executive seated across the bench from them whispered to a friend, "Will I ever find a man who will love me like that?"

The stress finally became too much. Richard resigned his post as president of the college. The school's trustees were horrified at the idea of losing his leadership. They offered to pay for Mary's full-time care so that Richard could continue on in his work. Friends told him he should simply pay for her to move into a nursing home so he could "get on with" his ministry.

Richard steadfastly, quietly refused. He gently reminded people of the words he had spoken before God forty-two years before: "In sickness and in health, to love and to cherish until we are parted by death."

So he resigned and took care of Mary, his soul mate, full-time. In his letter of resignation, Richard wrote,

"There is duty, there is fairness, there is integrity but there is more: I love Mary. She is a delight to me . . . I don't have to care for her. I get to! It is a high honor to care for so wonderful a person."

As the years passed, Alzheimer's slowly locked away parts of Mary, one piece at a time. And it thereby shut down a part of Richard at the same time. Eventually, Mary no longer knew who he was. But ironically, as her deterioration continued, Richard's love for her deepened, slowly seeping into every opening of his soul.

Yes, he would lose patience. Yes, he would get lonely. Yes, he would find frustration. But something stronger, something deeper, something greater sustained him.

He leaned on his family and friends. He relied on the memories he and Mary had built for years. Most of all, he drank deeply from the love of God.

After a lifetime of loving and serving God, Richard learned to praise him when days got their darkest and hope faded. Praise brought relief to his heavy, tired soul.

Unable to communicate in the final years, Mary died at the age of eighty-one, after twenty-five years of slowly slipping away. Richard was there, his love for her nourished by the love God had for them both.

_____

Better Every Day

11.1
11.2
11.3
11.4
11.5

Are You Paying Attention?

If you were to spend any time with a successful business, you would quickly discover that the very best companies measure everything. They have a fundamental understanding that if you don't measure it, you won't change it. This lesson tells us a lot about the human person and has huge implications for marriage.

Give your relationship a score between 1 and 10. You can define for yourself how you have come up with that number. There aren't any rules for what it means to be a 1 and what it means to be a 10. You aren't sharing the information with anyone; there is no need to be overly scientific about it. You will know if you are an 8 and you will know if you are a 2. And then you can think through why you settled on a particular number.

I suspect you have never been asked to rate your relationship in this way, just as most people aren't asked to rate their marriages in this way either. Everyone wants to have a great marriage, and of course we all say we want our marriage to get better every day. But we never stop and pay attention to how we are actually doing.

Do you have a better marriage and relationship this year than you did last year?

Every married couple should spend regular time with this question. As human beings we have a great need to know we are making progress, that things are getting better. And so finding ways to measure progress is critical, even in an area like marriage, which can be difficult to measure.

This simple question is a great way to start a conversation about your marriage. If you have to think very hard about it, you probably aren't paying enough attention to whether your marriage is better or worse.

Simply asking the question opens us up to a new realization about marriage. Our marriages—like our health, our finances, our relationships, and every other aspect of our lives—do not remain stagnant. Perhaps this moment of introspection leads to the conclusion that our marriage is not as strong as we thought it was. On the other hand, it may bring us to the realization that even though our marriage is very strong, there are great opportunities for it to grow even stronger. Regardless of what conclusions the exercise leads to, a key lesson here is that it is important to pay attention. Measuring helps us do that.

Giving your marriage a score between 1 and 10 is not scientific. But if you are honest with yourself and score yourself each month for a year, you will find your marriage improving. Measurement creates awareness, awareness leads to intentionality, and intentionality drives behavior.

It goes without saying that we want our marriages to get better every year, but there may be times in your life when your marriage is certainly not better than it was a year ago. Sometimes outside stressors cause a marriage to suffer. These stressors—the death of a family member or the loss of a job, for example—can create a circumstance in which improvement takes a backseat to mere survival. And that's OK. When you experience circumstances like this in your life, do not be disappointed that your marriage has not improved. Celebrate instead that it survived. This is a win in itself.

When you encounter these kinds of stressors, remember to just keep your eye on the ball. Press on. Keep moving forward. Don't let yourself get discouraged, and don't let yourself get distracted. It's easy to allow your attention to be diverted—to not see where things are better, and to overlook the little victories in the face of difficult circumstances.

So pay attention to your marriage. Notice when and how it is improving, notice the opportunities to make things better, and notice when it is the bedrock of your life.

Exercise:

Do you have a better relationship this year than you did last year?

A successful
marriage is
an edifice that
must be rebuilt
every day.

—André Maurois

Better Every Day

11.1
11.2
11.3
11.4
11.5

Don't Try to Do Everything

Virtue lies at the heart of any thriving marriage. Why?

Two virtuous people will always have a better relationship than two people without virtue. Two patient people will always have a better relationship than two impatient people. Two humble people will always have a better relationship than two proud people. Not sometimes, but every single time. If you are both striving to live virtuous lives, your relationship will prosper. But when you give up striving for virtue, your relationship will disintegrate.

This isn't true just for some people; it's true for all people. It isn't true just some of the time; it is true all of the time. Virtue lies at the heart of every great and thriving relationship.

Think of it this way. Who would you prefer as your employees or colleagues—men and women of virtue or those riddled with vice and selfishness? Would you prefer your neighbors be patient or impatient? Would you rather your extended family were generous or self-serving?

The whole world prefers virtue.

The world changes for the better only when men and women grow in virtue and character. In the same way, your marriage will grow and improve only when you and your future husband or wife grow in virtue and character. Less virtue can never lead to a better marriage. So how do we grow in virtue?

First off, it's important to get really clear on what virtue is. Virtue is "a habitual and firm disposition to do good" (CCC 1833). The Church teaches that seven foundational virtues form the corner-stone of the moral life. This foundation is made up of the three supernatural virtues (Faith, Hope, and Love) and the four cardinal virtues (Prudence, Justice, Temperance, and Fortitude). The three supernatural virtues free us from self-centeredness and protect us from the ultimate vice—pride—as they guide us to a relationship with God. The four cardinal virtues allow us to acquire the self-mastery necessary to make us free and capable of love.

It's important here to understand that no man or woman is born virtuous. Virtue must be sought out and can be acquired only by continual practice. You learn to ride a bicycle by riding a bicycle. You learn to play baseball by playing baseball. You learn to be patient by practicing patience.

And you become virtuous by practicing virtue.

The game changer for most people is simply becoming aware of the role of virtue in their lives and becoming intentional about growing in virtue. Awareness and intentionality will awaken you to the countless opportunities in your daily life to practice it.

Try picking one virtue and focusing only on that one virtue for a month. Perhaps you choose patience. For one month, make it your personal goal to show patience when the opportunity arises. Don't try to do everything. Don't try to do ten things. Just pick one virtue.

One of the great things about virtue is that the virtues are all inter-connected. When you grow in one, the others naturally improve as well. You can't become more patient without growing in kindness, love, and every other virtue. So don't worry about doing too little. The connection between virtue and the flourishing of a marriage is unquestionable.

Virtue lies at the heart of any thriving marriage.

Exercise:

What do you feel God is saying to you in this section?

....
....
....
....
....
....
....
....
....
....
....
....
....
....
....
....
....
....
....
....
....
....
....
....
....
....
....
....
....
....

The person who does not decide to love forever will find it very difficult to really love for even one day.

—St. John Paul II

Better Every Day

11.1

11.2

11.3

11.4

11.5

Small Is Beautiful and Powerful

My heart ached with a mixture of love and sadness as I flipped through the old photos: the first time she put bare feet on the grass, the first time she picked up a book, falling asleep with her in my arms.

Flipping through photos of the first few years of my oldest daughter's life, I couldn't help but smile. But at the same time I knew I could never go back there. I could never hold her again like she was a baby. I could never pull her around in a wagon. She was older now, and it was easy for me to imagine her ready to leave home for some new adventure.

One of the biggest mistakes we make as parents is wishing our kids were older. I remember for the first few years of my daughter's life wishing she was just a bit older. Wishing she could eat solid food. Wishing she could walk. Wishing she could use the bathroom on her own.

So many times I wished she was further along in her development, even though every parent I ever spoke to told me not to wish those years away. They'll be over too quick, they said. You'll wish you could come back to this time, they said.

One of our greatest failings as human beings is our inability to be present in our own lives.

So often we want things to happen right away, in the biggest way possible, so we can move on to the next thing.

God wants us to learn one of life's most important lessons: the power is in the little things. The laughter of a child. The sound of your spouse sleeping peacefully next to you. Sipping coffee and talking about your day. God wants us to have the best possible marriage. But bigger and faster doesn't necessarily mean better.

Life is a journey. God wants you to enjoy it. As you set out to have a thriving marriage, enjoy the journey. If you do not enjoy life, you will be no good to anybody, let alone your spouse.

A thriving marriage is not a victory to be won—it is a journey.

The journey of life isn't lived in the bigger and the faster. It's lived in the little things. If you decide to become a marathon runner, you don't go out and try to run a marathon straightaway. You start by running one mile a day, then over time you build yourself up. As you develop, you extend the distance. Many victories are won before a marathon runner's first race. Every mile is a powerful victory.

Life and marriage are a marathon, not a sprint. Small victories are the key. Little by little. This is the greatness of the human spirit. Small victories, one upon another, are the making of every great marriage. The small victories build confidence, help you both become the-best-version-of-yourselves, and set you on the path to a thriving and life-giving marriage.

As the famous saying goes, "Every day, in every way, I'm getting better and better."

Let this be the anthem for your life and your marriage. Every day, in every way, get a little bit better.

The path to a great marriage, great faith, great finances, and a great life goes through the little things. St. Thérèse of Lisieux embodied this best of all. She had a great desire to be a saint, but she knew she wasn't capable of great feats. She would not cure cancer or found a university. She was just a small and quiet girl, living in a convent, with nothing special to offer the world. She died at only twenty-four years old. But she discovered the power of doing little things with incredible love. By taking every small task or conversation each day and offering it to God as a prayer, she slowly grew ever holier. And she shared with the world her "Little Way."

St. Thérèse demonstrated the power of little things in your spiritual life. A few minutes a day devoted to prayer changes your soul over time, just as the incoming tide changes the coastline not in a single day but over the years. Reading the daily Gospel from Mass reshapes your mind slowly but surely. Focus on the little things and let the power of faith transform your life.

God invites you to experience the power of the little things. If you cannot find peace in the journey, you will not find peace in the destination. Be present in your own life. It is an amazing and rare gift to your marriage.

Exercise:

Write down five little things you love about each other. Maybe it's a look you give or something you always say. Maybe it's some little thing you do for each other. Make a list and put it on your bathroom mirror after your wedding to help remind both of you of the power of the little things.

Be present in
your own life.

11.1

11.2

Better Every Day

11.3

11.4

11.5

One Small Step

By now you have probably come to the conclusion that there are some changes you would like to make in various aspects of your life. To be honest, God's dream has shown me there are some very specific ways I wish to grow.

What matters is what you do next. If you feel like there are changes you want to make to yourself and to your relationship, I am so excited for you. Incredible possibilities lie ahead for you. Dynamic Catholic is dedicated to helping you in this journey, and we hope to give you the tools you need to have an incredible life and marriage.

Wherever you are in the journey, you may be thinking that you just don't have time for anything else. The principle of continuous improvement is about to become your new best friend. All this principle asks you to do is to take one small step, and it can be applied to almost any area of your life. Making small daily investments usually leads to large returns.

Here are some examples of where you can apply the principle of continuous improvement: losing weight, paying off debt, improving your marriage, running long distances, or simply reading the Bible. Programs that ask people to make radical, sweeping changes fail most of the time. Examples include diets that require you to cut out all your favorite foods at once or giving up an addiction cold turkey. Some people succeed in these programs, but the great majority fail. Most of us need a gentler path.

Sometimes Catholicism can seem like one of those rigid, all-or-nothing plans. We need to find small, simple ways for people to explore the faith and grow. It is true that God sometimes calls us to take a great leap. But most of the time he invites us to make small, continuous improvements.

Psychologists often use this method masterfully. In one case a patient who was tremendously overweight was asked to stand on the treadmill for one minute each morning. Just stand there!

Another with the same problem but who was also addicted to television was simply asked to stand up and march in front of the television for one minute each hour. Their doctors noticed the attitude of each had changed.

The suggested change was so small and nonthreatening that they started to think, "I can do that," whereas in the past everything they had been told they needed to do seemed so far out of reach that they shut down and did nothing.

Change in its smallest, least threatening form is usually the most successful.

Let's consider the elements of a thriving marriage you've already discussed: dreaming together, expectations, spirituality, sexuality, family, money, and forgiveness. You may be saying to yourself that you have a full, hectic life, that there is no way you can fit in all the possible improvements you see. That may be true. But could you spend one dinner conversation in the next week talking to your future spouse about your dreams? Or could you set an alarm and vow to say an Our Father for each other each day at the same time?

One small step! Nobody is so busy that they cannot set aside one minute for a quick prayer for their spouse each day. It is just one small, seemingly insignificant step. But if you practice it with discipline, you will be amazed how that one minute impacts your marriage.

Would you take one small step if. . .
. . . you believed it would lead to an incredible marriage?
. . . you thought it would lead you to a dynamic spiritual life?
. . . you knew it would inspire the people around you?

BETTER TOGETHER is about taking that next small step.

Every day God invites you to take one small step toward a better marriage.

There is no such thing as overnight success.

We have shared many ideas and practices with you. Your job is to find the one small step you should be focusing on at the moment and apply it to your life and your relationship. You may need to go through the sessions several times to really absorb what you have learned. But each time you come back, focus on the one small step that best suits you and your mate at that time in your life. And be sure to take note of the progress you have made.

Most people who have accomplished anything worthwhile in their lives will tell you that when they look back, it all happened little by little. There is no such thing as overnight success. Life unfolds little by little, in incremental steps.

Whatever it is for you, I pray you will have the courage to take it.

Pray Together:

ST. AUGUSTINE'S PRAYER TO THE HOLY SPIRIT

Breathe in me, O Holy Spirit,
That my thoughts may all be holy.
Act in me, O Holy Spirit,
That my work, too, may be holy.
Draw my heart, O Holy Spirit,
That I love but what is holy.
Strengthen me, O Holy Spirit,
To defend all that is holy.
Guard me, then O Holy Spirit,
That I may always be holy.
Amen

Better Every Day

11.1

11.2

11.3

11.4

11.5

Stuck in the Mud

I once heard an interview with an international ultramarathon champion who had just come off a first-place female finish in a race. This woman would compete in races consisting of a two-mile swim, hundred-mile bike ride, and twenty-five-mile run, all in one day.

She described her training regimen. Up at four a.m. daily, over six hours of training every day, and a ten-thousand-calorie, six-meal diet. My jaw dropped listening to her run through a typical training day hour by hour. It seemed impossible. It left me feeling bewildered.

One of the greatest mistakes we can make in looking at the successful is thinking it's easy for them. It doesn't matter if we are talking about a world-champion ultramarathoner, a successful entrepreneur, or even a couple with an incredible marriage. The trap is to think that they don't face the same challenges we do.

Take training, for example. I was surprised to hear this world champion share how much she hates getting up that early in the morning. She talked about how many days she wishes she could just sit on the couch and watch television in her sweatpants instead of training. It's so easy to assume that these temptations don't exist for someone like her.

But she faces the same feelings as everyone else. What really sets the successful apart is their ability to get through those feelings and press on.

The same is true for every thriving marriage you witness. It's easy to think, "Yeah, well, of course they have a thriving marriage. They don't have the problems I have. They don't have the challenges I do. Of course their marriage is great! It's easy for them!" But any amount of examination shows that this simply isn't true.

It doesn't matter who you are, you are going to face difficulties in your marriage. And even the best couples—the ones who are committed to continuous improvement and focused on the little things— are going to feel like they are stuck in the mud from time to time.

During that time, you'll be tempted to think that you must do something monumental to get out of it.

At one point during the interview, this world champion ultramarathoner shared how she makes sure she gets out of bed every morning. She revealed the small steps she takes to beat resistance on those mornings when she just doesn't feel like getting out of bed. Her secret: She just focuses on getting her shoes on. In fact, she doesn't even wear socks when she trains, so that there is one less step to success. She wakes up, swings her feet over the side of the bed, where her shoes have been set the night before, and slips them on—immediately. Right away. That way, even when she doesn't feel like doing it, she's already taken a small step in the right direction before she has even really woken up.

Instead, figure out ways to focus on just "putting on your shoes" when you feel like your marriage is stuck in the mud. An excellent example of the power of these little acts comes from relationship expert Dr. John Gottman.

Through observing couples over the course of thirty years, Dr. Gottman has arrived at a 5:1 ratio that helps him predict with 94 percent accuracy the probability of a couple's long-term marital success or failure. The ratio is simple: five positive interactions for every negative interaction.

Every eye roll, shrug, or sarcastic remark needs to be offset with five positive gestures: an affectionate touch, a listening nod, caring remark, smile, a small act of kindness, or shared laughter. This ratio is so important that Dr. Gottman's motto for making marriage last is "Small things often." These small acts help you keep tenderness and affection alive and well in your relationship. More important, they help you simply be grateful for each other and the blessing of having each other in your lives.

One powerful way for couples to break out when they feel stuck in the mud is through a simple thirty-day focus. For

My husband and I recently went to the Passion and Purpose seminar in Arizona. I cannot even begin to describe the transformation that has occurred in both of us. Prior to the seminar (even minutes) we were struggling to even be in the same room together. Our hearts were so hurt and guarded. This event truly transformed our hearts and healed us from within. It has reminded us that our relationship is not just a marriage; it's a sacrament. We were able to forgive and want to have a wonderful marriage not only with ourselves, but with God. Thank you to your ministry for answering God's call to share and guide others to a strong Catholic marriage. Intentions for our marriage to continue to strengthen in Christ and in each other would be appreciated. Thank you and God bless you.

—Attendee Couple at Dynamic Catholic Passion and Purpose for Marriage Event 2017

thirty days, start and end each day with a small, positive act of kindness for your spouse. Maybe it's making the bed. Maybe it's getting up early and making the coffee. Maybe it is a simple kind sentence: "I'm glad we get to live this day together." Just one little thing first thing in the morning. Then at the end of the day, perhaps you simply look your husband directly in the eyes and say, "I love you." Or you give your wife a long foot rub before she goes to sleep. Just one little thing at the end of the day. This thirty-day focus helps you break free from that feeling of being stuck. The power is in the little things!

Exercise:

What do you sense that God is saying to you in this section?

....
....
....
....
....
....
....
....
....
....
....
....
....
....
....
....
....
....

Additional Resources

What the Church, the Bible, and the Saints Teach
Us About the Sacrament of Marriage

Love That Flows Every Day

Marriage between two baptized persons is a sacrament. That's why the Church teaches that the couple's relationship expresses in a unique way the unbreakable bond of love between Christ and his people. Like the other six sacraments of the Church, marriage is a sign that reveals Jesus and through which his love is communicated. Jesus instituted all seven sacraments and entrusted them to the Church to be celebrated in faith. The liturgy, rituals, and prayers at your wedding express visibly what God is doing invisibly in the two of you.

In a sacramental marriage, God's love becomes present to the spouses in their total union. That love then also flows through them to their family and their community.

CATECHISM

1605 The woman, "flesh of his flesh," his equal, his nearest in all things, is given to him by God as a "helpmate"; she thus represents God from whom comes our help.

SCRIPTURE

For this reason I bow my knees before the Father, from whom every family in heaven and on earth takes its name. I pray that, according to the riches of his glory, he may grant that you may be strengthened in your inner being with power through his Spirit, and that Christ may dwell in your hearts through faith, as you are being rooted and grounded in love. I pray that you may have the power to comprehend, with all the saints, what is the breadth and length and height and depth, and to know the love of Christ that surpasses knowledge, so that you may be filled with all the fullness of God.

Now to him who by the power at work within us is able to accomplish abundantly far more than all we can ask or imagine, to him be glory in the church and in Christ Jesus to all generations, forever and ever. Amen.
(Ephesians 3:14–21)

SAINT

In the light of Mary, the Church sees in the face of women the reflection of a beauty which mirrors the loftiest sentiments of which the human heart is capable: the self-offering totality of love; the strength that is capable of bearing the greatest sorrows; limitless fidelity and tireless devotion to work; the ability to combine penetrating intuition with words of support and encouragement.
—St. John Paul II

Notes

On the

Love is beautiful when it's professed, but
it's only meaningful when it's practiced.

—Brené Brown

On the Day

SESSION 12

Wisdom for Success from Anniversaries

I've always been fascinated by couples who have been married a long time. So, every new couple I meet, I ask them what has been their secret to longevity.

I met one couple at their seventieth wedding anniversary party, and asked the wife, "What's the secret to being married seventy years?"

She quickly responded, "Neither one of us died."

On another occasion, I listened to a couple on the radio discuss their seventy-fifth anniversary. The announcer asked the wife, "What's the secret to being married seventy-five years?"

She paused and said, "I always let him have my way."

And of course, earlier in BETTER TOGETHER, you remember the story of John and Amelia Rocchio, who, when they had been married eighty-two years, made the newspaper. They lived outside Providence, Rhode Island. He was 101; she was ninety-nine.

At the time, their anniversary made them the longest-married couple in America.

When the reporter asked John, "What's the secret to being married eighty-two years?"

John simply replied, "Patience."

This is true wisdom from those who have succeeded in marriage and done the work of becoming better together.

———————————

I . . . urge you to live in a manner worthy of the call you have received, with all humility and gentleness, with patience, bearing with one another through love.

(Ephesians 4:1–2)

We prepare for every-thing we consider to be important.

___

On the Day

The Blur

The Day. You've probably already begun calling it that. It has become the focus of your thoughts, your schedule, and your mind at this point. The Day. Your wedding day. All the planning. All the details. Who to invite, what your mother wants to include, what your mother-in-law doesn't want to include, what kind of food, who will wear what, what time your aunt arrives from Ohio, what kind of flowers to use on the tables, and the list grows and grows.

In the middle of all the hullaballoo, I want to suggest one thought:

Know how your best days begin, and begin your wedding day that way.

With all the wisdom (and opinions) people are going to give you about the Day, that one thought is all I want to share.

Know how your best days begin, and begin your wedding day that way.

Because if you do that, at the end of the day, you will be grateful. I am not sure I can even begin to describe for you how fast the Day goes.

I mean, for me, one minute, it's 12am and I'm lying there wondering if I'm ever going to fall asleep because oh my gosh, I'm getting married tomorrow! Then, next thing I know, I'm walking down the aisle with my dad, trying not to trip over my dress, beaming at the very handsome man at the end of the aisle. Flash forward and my new husband and I are on our red-eye flight for our honeymoon. The day is going to go by so fast, guys.

I mean, it's crazy.

And if you want to make the most of the Day, after all the thought, planning, and frenzy you've invested, be intentional about this one thought.

Know how your best days begin, and begin your wedding day that way.

How do your best days begin? Think about it for a moment. Think about the past month—on your really good days, how did they begin? Maybe with some quiet time or some prayer? With a good cup of coffee, perhaps? With a long list of stuff to do already prepared so that you could enter the day clearheaded and focused? With daily Mass early in the morning? Possibly with a long walk with your dog?

Take a moment and write it down. How did your best days begin?

Now think about how you can begin the Day in that same way. Because it is going to sweep by you if you're not careful, and you want to be sure to invest yourself intentionally on a day as big as this.

Great days usually start the night before. If you really want to create a great day, you will probably want to start the night before; that's how great days usually start. With some good sleep. With a light meal. Without too much craziness or excessive eating, drinking, or decibels. Those are often good days in themselves and probably need their own plans, but they likely do not have any place on the night before your wedding. Guys, feel free to find a time to go out and be crazy. To some extent, that is OK. But do it the *night before* the night before.

You want to be fully present on the Day. After all, it is a big day. The sacrament of marriage. You're performing it yourself. The priest is only there to assist you. You're going to welcome people from every facet of your life: childhood, family, school, work, parish, all of them. You're giving yourself publicly and completely to your new spouse. You're beginning your own family. You're launching into one of life's greatest adventures. It's a big day. You'll want to be focused and fully present. Of all days, on this one, you will want to be fully alive.

By this time in your preparation, our hope is that you have built a routine of daily prayer. The night before and the morning of your wedding are two times to take advantage of that to the fullest. How are you going to prepare prayerfully? Pray for your future spouse before you go to bed.

It will help to have a plan for the Day. Who do you want to be sure to have a personal, uninterrupted moment with, a moment just for you? What special ritual or tradition will you want to make the most of? When will you do that and with whom? What emotions do you think you will be feeling the night before and who will help you manage those emotions well? Who will aggravate those emotions? Who will you want to hang out with the night before so that you make the most of that special time?

Great days start the night before.

Have a plan for the Day.

Be intentional.

Don't sweat the small stuff. No need to get in a dither about little stuff no one will notice anyway. Because if you give in to that temptation, the whirlwind will sweep you away. And nobody wants that to happen on the Day.

So let me remind you one more time: Know how your best days begin, and begin your wedding day that way.

Great days start the night before.

Exercise:

Who are three people you want to have a meaningful moment with on the day of your wedding?

_____
_____
_____
_____
_____
_____
_____
_____
_____
_____
_____
_____
_____
_____
_____
_____
_____
_____
_____
_____
_____
_____
_____
_____
_____
_____
_____
_____
_____
_____

Love that leads
to marriage is
a gift from God
and a great act of
faith toward other
human beings.

—St. John Paul II

How One Couple Prepared the Day Before

Written by Kathryn, a Dynamic Catholic Ambassador and a Bridesmaid

Kati and TJ wanted to do everything they could to make sure their wedding day was exceptional, and they knew that wouldn't happen by accident. So they were intentional with three specific choices to ensure it was everything they dreamed it would be.

First, they hosted a modest rehearsal dinner for their parents and the bridal party. It was intimate and simple. They served pizza and wine, everyone had a chance to laugh and share stories, and the night ended early. This isn't to say that every rehearsal dinner has to be this way, but for Kati and TJ, it was the perfect way to start the next day.

Second, they prayed together in the same way they did (and still do) every night. Kati and TJ had developed a habit of alternating who leads prayer every night, always thanking God for the gift of the day and ending in an Our Father. By keeping their same routine the night before the wedding, they kept themselves focused on what mattered most and infused a sense of calm and routine into the most important day of their lives.

Last, Kati and TJ decided to focus on how they were present to those around them on their wedding day. So at ten a.m. on the wedding day, Kati handed her phone off to her maid of honor, who would take care of any texts, calls, and emails that needed to be answered. TJ did the same thing. This way, they would be free to fully experience each moment of the day.

Kati and TJ impressed all of their wedding guests with their relaxed demeanors and the amount of time they were able to devote to each family member, friend, and coworker who attended the wedding. By choosing to be intentional about their wedding day, they ensured that it was everything they dreamed it would be.

On the Day

12.1

12.2

12.3

12.4

12.5

The Day

We prepare for everything we consider to be important.
You wouldn't show up to run a marathon and expect to finish if you hadn't been training. We don't expect to excel in exams if we haven't studied. Preparation is essential for any great experience.

And you've been preparing for a while now. You've been preparing all the details of the Day. And you've been preparing yourselves to be better together for life.

There are two types of preparation: the temporal and the spiritual. A lot of your preparation has been invested in the temporal things of flowers, music, and invitations.

If nothing else, the last hours before your wedding should have a prayerful spirit. The temporal has already been well prepared; the spiritual preparation should take precedence in the last hours.

Nick, my husband, and I discovered up front that you'll probably never have the chance again to have such small decisions offend so many people in such big ways. Though we certainly wanted to consider the feelings of our guests, we ultimately knew that our day was about our marriage together. So we made the day our own.

What did this actually look like? For me, I hired a friend to make our bouquets by using flowers from a local grocery store—and the bouquets looked awesome. Making the day our own also meant carefully choosing our Mass readings together, studying and praying through them together prior to our wedding day. It also meant creating a step-by-step guide to the Mass so that our non-Catholic friends and family members could understand the significance of what was happening to Nick and me.

It was a beautiful day and it was exactly what we wanted it to be. So I will say this to you again: the day can look however you want it to look.

From sunrise on the Day all the way through to the ceremony, it is a very different experience for men compared to women. For women this is often a well-thought-out dream that may have been carefully planned since you were a little girl. But for many of the guys, you just show up when you are told to show up and do what you are told to do. The bride's day can be overrun with details and commitments and people, while the groom's day can often be a long day of boring waiting. No matter the circumstances, you are both going to have very different days before you meet at the altar.

So, I have just one more thought:

The Day can look however you want it to look.

I know, you're thinking, "You have no idea how many people want to have a say or even control the Day for me." I get it. I've been there.

But I will say it again: The Day can look however you want it to look. You and your spouse-to-be are the drivers of this train. Do not let anyone try to take that from you. This is the Day, your day. Not that it's all about you—but it is all about the two of you and what you are inviting God to be a part of as you embark together. This is your sacrament with him. This day belongs to the three of you—you, your mate, and God.

Your wedding day isn't just a party. It's a celebration of what God is doing in your life. The joining of two hearts, the coming together of two lives. This is the day you've dreamed of, the person you've dreamed of being with.

If you're driving the train, you get to decide when it leaves, how fast it travels, and where it is going. Just because the makeup artist wants to start at 6:30am doesn't mean you have to. Just because the photographer wants to do all of his stuff beforehand doesn't mean it has to be that way.

Five ways for the groom to spend the day of the wedding (other than golfing and drinking beer and showing up sunburnt at the church):

1. Visiting with out-of-town family members and guests

2. Attending Mass or adoration with his groomsmen to pray for his fiancée and their life together

3. Playing basketball with friends to burn off tension

4. Taking a long walk to collect himself

5. Looking at old pictures with his father and giving thanks for those who have made this day possible

Ultimately, this is your day. Your sacrament. Yours with God.

The Day should play out the way you want it to play out. Of course, you will want to find ways to honor important people in your life. You don't want to be self-indulgent. But don't let other people's expectations prevent you from mapping out the day you believe God wants for your marriage. And that may mean you have to stand up for each other.

Prayer is a gift that helps us be in the present moment. Prayer teaches us to be fully present to whoever is in front of us right now and whatever we are doing right now. Prayer slows things down, giving weight and meaning to every interaction. Anything and everything can be a prayer: getting your hair done, listening to a toast, greeting friends at their table during the reception. So let your prayer life help you achieve the worthy goal of staying present throughout the day to each setting you're in and to each person you're with.

This is what your wedding day is. It's a collection of moments and a collection of people. All the people God has put in your life come together and help you experience the life-changing power of his dream for your life. You are no longer two, but one. You are no longer man and woman, but husband and wife.

This day is about the two of you and God's dream for your life together.

For guidance on planning a great day down to the last detail, get your copy of The Wedding Planning Book by Dynamic Catholic.

On the Day

12.1

12.2

12.3

12.4

12.5

The Ceremony

If you already know that the Day is going to fly by, then the ceremony can be nothing more than a speed bump if you're not careful. It'll be just something that you slow down for, but then proceed to drive right over.

But this is the sacrament. This is the focal point of the whole day, the whole weekend. In many ways, you've thought through every moment. You know what your perfect day looks like.

You may have been looking forward to this moment your entire life. So, here is one more thought I offer you:

Do. Not. Miss. It.

This is your sacramental moment. It is beautiful. Friends and family have gathered to celebrate with you and to pray for you. God is binding the two of you together and creating something new. Two are becoming one. Don't miss it. This is special.

You can use key moments throughout the wedding day to refocus on what matters most. A remarkable act of God is occurring all around you. Every so often, take a step back and soak in the grace and love all around you.

Let's call those opportunities "refocus moments."

Here are a few ways to do just that:

1. The morning is probably going to be a flurry of getting ready, taking pictures, and seeing people. Before the wedding ceremony begins, refocus. Find a few moments of quiet. Pray. This will help calm your spirit and focus you before the big moment.

2. The doors open. Your bride walks down the aisle. Everyone turns to look. What are you

thinking about? Refocus. Think about what attracted you to her, why you are choosing to marry her and her alone. Give thanks for the dreams you both have. Gaze at her and give thanks.

3. As you walk down the aisle, look at the people around you. A room filled with love. Refocus. God loves you and there is nothing you can do about it! That is good news. Love abounds in your life. And now your husband-to-be awaits you. Love.

4. In the Mass, when you say, "Christ, have mercy," refocus. For just a moment, recognize you are both imperfect people. But God will be your strength and your guide. Give thanks.

5. When you exchange your vows, say the words slowly. Refocus. You are giving yourself completely for life. The old is passing away. Something new is emerging. Love is not a feeling; it's a choice. This is special.

6. As you receive the Eucharist, refocus. This is a special moment. God's Body and Blood bind the entire Church together. And yet he knows and holds each of you by name. He will nourish you for the rest of your life together.

7. In your first moment alone before the reception, refocus. Pause and take a deep breath together. Look into each other's eyes and smile at what has just taken place. God has taken the two of you and made you one. Give thanks.

When it comes to your ceremony, go deeper with Dynamic Catholic's book, *Planning a Great Wedding Ceremony*.

Rejoice always, pray without ceasing, give thanks in all circumstances; for this is the will of God in Christ Jesus for you.

(1 Thessalonians 5:16–18)

Exercise:

How do you plan to refocus on what matters most—God and his love for you both—on the Day itself?

....
....
....
....
....
....
....
....
....
....
....
....
....
....
....
....
....
....
....
....
....
....
....
....
....
....
....
....

How One Couple Reminded Everyone at Their Wedding That Marriage Is a Sacrament

Written by Mark, a Dynamic Catholic Ambassador and an attendee at the wedding Mass

I remember talking to my wife on the way home that evening about how the ceremony reflected Claire's and Jake's love for Jesus, as much as their love for each other. It was so authentic and refreshing, I don't think I ever left a wedding with such a strong impression.

From the Scripture readings to the lyrics of the songs they selected, you couldn't help but feel you were witnessing a sacrament, not just a wedding. Here are nine ways they made it feel that way.

1. Everyone participated at Mass. Claire and Jake were very intentional about picking hymns that matched the readings. They also wrote their own petitions.
2. Jake and Claire both had their attending parties pray over them just before Mass started.
3. Their godparents brought up the gifts.
4. They asked their priest to request that everyone—even non-Catholics—come up to Communion for a blessing.
5. Claire and Jake were the Eucharistic ministers for the Body, and the priests gave the cup. That way, they got to see all their guests and give them Communion.
6. A bridesmaid sent prayers to the family and bridal party for use in the days leading up to the wedding.
7. At the end of Mass, Claire and Jake joyfully sang "How Can I Keep from Singing" as they walked back down the aisle.
8. At the reception, everyone was able to select a virtue in William Bennett's *The Children's Book of Virtues* and write a note next to it in the book—a cool memory for Claire and Jake to recall as they read the book to their children in years to come. That way, when they read stories to their children, they will be filled with notes from the people who were still praying for and supporting their marriage and family.
9. Finally, Jake and Claire gave out Dynamic Catholic books as a wedding favor to everyone at the reception—a gift with a special faith-filled mission focus for everyone to leave with.

On the Day

12.1

12.2

12.3

12.4

12.5

The Reception

When you are planning something, a great place to start is with a question: **What is the purpose?**

It's amazing how asking that one simple question can bring things into a clear focus. Purpose. In other words, what are we hoping to achieve?

So let me ask you a crazy question. What's the purpose of your reception?

Why are you doing it?

The purpose of a wedding reception—which can come in as many different forms as there are couples—is to celebrate the incredible sacrament that just took place with all the people who have helped you get to this day and who will continue to pray for you through-out your marriage. We live in a culture that sometimes perverts this into way more than it needs to be. This shouldn't be stressful; this should be a gift for you, your guests, and your family.

Let's assume for a moment that you haven't already made all your plans. Who's going to decide what the reception is going to actually be like?

You're driving the train.

Are you making that decision as a couple? Or is it being made by the person with the checkbook? The caterer? The wedding planner? Who is going to decide?

Again, remember that you are the drivers of this train. You can take it wherever you want it to go. Too many couples operate as if the train leaves the station once they are engaged, with no brakes and no engineer. The train just goes and the bride and groom are passengers all the way at the back of the caboose.

Worse, over the years our culture has started to exaggerate and overspend on weddings. It's likely that your grandparents' recep-tion had cake and punch in the parish hall after a morning Mass.

Your great-grandparents are lucky if they have a photo or two from their wedding day. Now we spend thousands of dollars on photo shoots. American weddings and receptions have frequently evolved into self-indulgent, extravagant spectacles inspired by the crazy expectations of bridezillas and wedding shows. Over the years we've started comparing ourselves to every wedding we've ever been to.

It is helpful to remember, or at least consider, that most couples in America spend less than ten thousand dollars on their entire wedding, and the average cost is less than thirty thousand. For all the high-priced weddings, you sometimes have to wonder if anyone on the train ever even paused to ask, "Why exactly are we spending all this money? And could we possibly use that money on something more valuable or meaningful, like a down payment on a home or paying off a student loan?"

Most people don't see the cost of the options that are before them. For example, on the toothpaste aisle of the grocery store, there may be thirty-one brands of toothpaste. Lots of choices. Lots of prices. But we often just go straight for the one we are familiar with.

In the same way, there are lots of ways to celebrate a wedding. Lots of options for parties, dinners, and receptions. So, go back to the question at the beginning. It is a helpful one to discuss together before the train leaves the station. Why are we having a reception?

Then you can decide the best way to achieve that. The day is about celebrating the beginning of a "we," and it should reflect who you are together. Help each other keep the main thing the main thing.

You're driving the train. After all, everyone else has had their day. This is yours.

And this is God's.

Exercise:

Five suggestions to consider as you make reception decisions:

1. Ask yourselves, "How can we think about this differently from everything the culture has thrown at us? What do we really want?" Be honest. Be bold.

2. Use the parish hall as a gift to your guests. They won't have to navigate and drive to another location to find the reception. The whole day stays in the church and keeps a spirit of reverence and devotion. And you save money. Triple win.

3. Find a way to honor parents and grandparents as a part of the celebration. Their love has helped to make this celebration possible. God loves it when we honor our mother and father. And your guests will be touched by your thoughtful kindness.

4. Say to your guests at the beginning of the celebration, "This reception is our gift to all of you. We are grateful for you and your love in our lives."

5. Ask yourselves, "What really is our budget? How much is reasonable to celebrate this and who are we helping and serving by doing so?" If you are thinking about spending a hundred thousand dollars, pause and have an honest conversation about whether that really is the best use of your money. Perhaps it is. Or perhaps the temptation to spend so much is merely coming from a desire to keep up with the Joneses. You may find a more satisfying way to use that sum that suits who you are rather than who others expect you to be.

On the Day

12.1

12.2

12.3

12.4

12.5

The Difference Between a Wedding and a Marriage

By now, you have made a lot of decisions. You've decided to marry your spouse. That was a big one. And you've planned your wedding. That's huge. So many decisions—hundreds, maybe even thousands of them, big and small. All just to get married on the Day.

Take a moment and think about all the time and energy you put into planning your wedding. At times, it was stressful. And in the end, it was hard work. But, as you know, this is about more than just one day. It's about the start of something new. It's about the rest of your life together.

So I invite you to spend the same amount of time and energy you spent this past year on planning the wedding on making your marriage strong in the coming year. Dynamic Catholic will be here to help, offering you free resources and tools to build the marriage you dream of.

It is my greatest joy in life to wake up next to Nick every morning, to do life with him as a team, and to know I can talk to him about anything.

A wedding is not a marriage, just like a cocoon is not a butterfly.

Once your wedding day is over, your thinking will turn to the marriage in a very real way. And you will quickly discover again one of the key points of this BETTER TOGETHER marriage resource: Marriage is hard, and it takes work.

Now, don't get me wrong. Marriage is a lot of fun. And it is a lot of joy.

But it is important to remember that your marriage also is going to face some times of sorrow and some moments of real suffering. It is true for every one of us and every one of our marriages. The good news is that the sorrow and the suffering will be easier to bear because you have each other for support.

As Christians, we are all witnesses to Jesus. In many ways, you and I are like billboards for Christianity. We represent the faith everywhere we go and in everything we do. Other people look at us and decide what they think about Catholics and Christians when they observe what we do and hear what we say.

Here's my point for you. As a married couple, you will now be witnesses to the basic goodness of marriage. We live in a culture that loves to make fun of marriage and even mock it. If you were the only married couple a young dating couple ever got to see, would you have something they wanted?

Our culture uses a lot of negative humor around marriage. The constant negativity can radically impact the view of marriage for people who do not really understand what it is. And once you are married, your life together (what you do and what you say) will be a testimony to the people around you (and to the culture) of what marriage really is and can be.

The two of you can speak for the goodness of marriage whether you are asked or not. The way you live, the way you treat each other, the way you serve and love together—all of these will speak to the world about what marriage is and who we Catholic Christians are. Speak positively of marriage when given the opportunity, especially when you hear others doing the opposite. You're now a billboard for Christianity and for marriage. Wear it well.

So, after this wonderful time you and I have shared, I simply remind you to stay at it—really stay at it—and you will discover that you truly are better together.

May God bless you and all that he has in store for you together.

Pray Together:

Lord
At last this day of days has come
We have been preparing
For days and years
This is the day of dreams

Thank you Lord
For the meeting of
Our hearts
Our lives
Our souls
All is yearning
All is hope

Come bless our lives
You who see into future ways
With your eternal wisdom
Protect our nights and days

Make our home
A place of joy
When storm clouds gather
Let no hurt destroy

May your angels
Find a home from Heaven
Therein
When days are sad
May we hear them sing

Bless us with children
Fulfilling our dream
Placed in your trusting
Our future unseen

May friends young and old
Cross this threshold to find
A sacred embrace
A welcome in kind

Lord of love
May we know
The gift of your Spirit
In times of strength
In times of sorrow

When hearts are strong
When hearts are hollow
Whisper courage to the wind

May the harvest of our lives
Mellow our hearts
Where silence is sacred
And words can depart
For you are there
Keeping watch
In our twilight years

This day is but the beginning
Of love in eternity
Beyond
Above
Below
How could we ever know
The depth of your love

Till death do us part. . .
What is death
Only finding love
Beyond the stars.

—Fr. Liam Lawton, from *The Hope Prayer*

On the Day

Additional Resources

What the Church, the Bible, and the Saints Teach
Us About the Sacrament of Marriage

Jesus and His First Miracle

In the Gospel of John, Jesus began his public ministry by attending a wedding feast in Cana with his mother, Mary. In fact, he performed his first miracle there: turning water into wine. His presence and actions provided a dignity and witness to the essential goodness of marriage.

CATECHISM

1613 On the threshold of his public life Jesus performs his first sign—at his mother's request—during a wedding feast. The Church attaches great importance to Jesus' presence at the wedding at Cana. She sees in it the confirmation of the goodness of marriage and the proclamation that thenceforth marriage will be an efficacious sign of Christ's presence.

SCRIPTURE

On the third day there was a wedding in Cana of Galilee, and the mother of Jesus was there. Jesus and his disciples had also been invited to the wedding. When the wine gave out, the mother of Jesus said to him, "They have no wine." And Jesus said to her, "Woman, what concern is that to you and to me? My hour has not yet come." His mother said to the servants, "Do whatever he tells you." Now standing there were six stone water jars for the Jewish rites of purification, each holding twenty or thirty gallons. Jesus said to them, "Fill the jars with water." And they filled them up to the brim. He said to them, "Now draw some out, and take it to the chief steward." So they took it. When the steward tasted the water that had become wine, and did not know where it came from (though the servants who had drawn the water knew), the steward called the bridegroom and said to him, "Everyone serves the good wine first, and then the inferior wine after the guests have become drunk. But you have kept the good wine until now." Jesus did this, the first of his signs, in Cana of Galilee, and revealed his glory; and his disciples believed in him.
(John 2:1–11)

SAINT

I also saw the holy city, a new Jerusalem coming down out of heaven from God, prepared as a bride adorned for her husband.
—St. John in Revelation 21:2

Notes

Notes